Gods and Goddesses

Discovering Mythology

To Bill, for seeing me through.
Thanks so much.
Wendy

Gods and Goddesses

Discovering Mythology

**Other titles in Lucent Books
Discovering Mythology series include:**

Death and the Underworld
Heroes
Quests and Journeys

Gods and Goddesses

by Wendy Mass

Lucent Books, Inc.
10911 Technology Place, San Diego, California 92127

On cover: A late Roman stonework depicts a sun god.

Library of Congress Cataloging-in-Publication Data

Mass, Wendy, 1967–
    Gods and goddesses / by Wendy Mass.
        p. cm. — (Discovering mythology)
Includes bibliographical references and index.
Summary: Examines the origins and nature of Egyptian, Hindu, Celtic, Greek, Roman,
Viking, and Aztec gods and goddesses as revealed in the mythologies of these cultures.
    ISBN 1-56006-852-3
    1. Gods—Juvenile literature. 2. Goddesses—Juvenile
literature. [1. Gods. 2. Goddesses. 3. Mythology.] I. Title. II. Series.
    BL473 .M375 2002
    291.2'11—dc21

2001005775

Printed in the U.S.A.

Contents

Foreword

Created by ancient cultures, the world's many and varied mythologies are humanity's attempt to make sense of otherwise inexplicable phenomena. Floods, drought, death, creation, evil, even the possession of knowledge—all have been explained in myth. The ancient Greeks, for example, observed the different seasons but did not understand why they changed. As a result, they reasoned that winter, a cold, dark time of year, was the result of a mother in mourning; the three months of winter were the days the goddess Demeter missed her daughter Persephone who had been tricked into spending part of her year in the underworld. Likewise, the people of India experienced recurring droughts, weeks and months during which their crops withered and their families starved. To explain the droughts, the Indians created the story of Vritra, a terrible demon who lived in the clouds and sucked up all the world's moisture. And the Vikings, in their search for an understanding of wisdom and knowledge, created Odin, their culture's most powerful god, who gave the world the gift of poetry and possessed two mythic ravens named Thought and Memory.

The idea of myth, fantastic stories that answer some of humanity's most enduring questions, spans time, distance, and differing cultural ideologies. Humans—whether living in the jungles of South America, along the rocky coasts of northern Europe, or on the islands of Japan—all formulated stories in an attempt to understand their world. And although their worlds differed greatly, they sometimes found similar ways of explaining the unknown or unexplainable events of their lives. Other times, there were differences, but the method of explanation—the myth—remains the same.

Each book in the Discovering Mythology series revolves around a specific topic—for example, death and the underworld; monsters; or heroes—and each chapter examines a selection of myths related to that topic. This allows young readers to note both the similarities and differences across cultures and time. Almost all cultures have myths to explain creation and death, for instance, but the actual stories sometimes vary widely. The Babylonians believed that the earth was the offspring of primordial parents, while the Navajo Indians of North America assert that the world emerged over time much like an infant grows into an adult. In ancient Greek mythology, a deceased person passed quickly into the underworld, a physical place that offered neither reward nor punishment for one's deeds in life. Egyptian myths, on the other hand, contended that a person's quality of existence in the afterlife, an ambiguous state of being, depended on his actions on earth.

In other cases, the symbolic creature or hero and what it represents are the same, but the purpose of the story may be different. Although monster myths in different cultures may not always explain the same phenomenon or offer insight into the same ethical quandary, monsters nearly always represent evil. The shape-shifting beast-men of ancient Africa represented the evils of trickery and wile. These vicious animal-like creatures transformed themselves into attractive, charming humans to entrap unsuspecting locals. Persia's White Demon devoured townspeople and nobles alike; it took the intelligence and strength of an extraordinary prince to defeat the monster and save the countryside. Even the Greek Furies, although committing their evil acts in the name of justice, were ugly, violent creatures who murdered people guilty of killing others. Only the goddess Athena could tame them.

The Discovering Mythology series presents the myths of many cultures in a format accessible to young readers. Fully documented secondary source quotes and numerous mythological tales enliven the text. Sidebars highlight interesting stories, creatures, and traditions. Annotated bibliographies offer ideas for further research. Each book in this engaging series provides students with a wealth of information as well as launching points for further discussion.

The Origins of the Gods

Swiss psychoanalyst Carl Jung once wrote, "If all the world's traditions were cut off at a single blow, the whole of mythology and the whole history of religion would start all over again with the next generation."[1] He was speaking from the viewpoint that mythology springs from a "collective unconscious," meaning people all over the world, from the beginning of humanity, have the same basic needs to fill and will keep filling them in the same ways.

To Jung, religion fills a primal need to understand the workings of the world. The study of ancient gods and goddesses reveals patterns in their development that actually vary very little from culture to culture and across great spans of time. One way to explain how gods are born is with an example about rain gods that, while overly simplistic, shows the basic process that fosters religion. Survival in primitive agricultural societies depended on adequate rainful: Without it, no crops would grow and people and animals could die. One day the rain stops falling and there is a drought, which creates much fear among the inhabitants of the land. Sooner or later it starts to rain again and the people are grateful. They praise the rain itself and thank it for providing them with sustenance. When another drought occurs, the people think, "We must have upset the rain, it is punishing us. Let us show our appreciation for it by leaving out offerings of food and wine." Then it rains again and the people believe the rain accepted their offerings and is rewarding them. When the rains stop again, the cycle repeats itself. Eventually, the spirit of the rain takes on a name and the people believe they understand why it rains.

The Pantheon

Like the rain spirit, the first gods were associated with nature and the creation of the world. By giving the forces of nature names and personalities, the people felt their lives were interconnected with these forces. They gained a greater sense of power and belonging, and the world around them was easier to interpret and less mysterious. If they assigned a god to carry the sun across the sky, they no longer had to wonder how or why the sun rose and set each day, and they could feel certain it would rise and set the next day.

After the development of the basic gods of nature, others followed rapidly. Almost every ancient pantheon includes a creator god, a sky god, a sun god, a rain god, a thunder god; a god of the sea, of fire, of war; a mother goddess, a moon god or goddess, a god/goddess of love, of fertility, and of death. There is virtually no limit to the aspects of life assigned to deities: wisdom, the arts, weaving, beginnings, endings, the hunt, the harvest, the fog, wine, sex, destruction—anything that a specific culture needed or valued.

Osiris, the Egyptian god of death. Many ancient cultures had gods for important aspects of life such as love, fertility, war, and death.

The hierarchy of the gods in each culture depended on the society itself. In a desert land, for instance, the rain god takes on much more importance and greater prominence than in a mountainous country, where people may place the god of the hunt atop their pantheon. By studying the gods and goddesses of a particular culture, historians can discern more about it and differentiate it from others. They learn what aspects of life were most important by seeing how the deities were ranked in the pantheon and how much power, if any, these supernatural authority figures had over the lives of the worshipers.

The Functions of Mythology

Mythology scholar Roni Jay offers many ways in which mythology functions in specific cultures. According to Jay, the gods are invoked

1. To explain natural phenomena

2. To control natural forces

3. To bind a society together under common supernatural leadership

4. To interpret historical events such as wars and natural disasters

5. To set examples for people's behavior

6. To justify a social structure

7. To control people [2]

Within the framework of these seven objectives, each society may have a different form of worship. In some cultures people felt

A giant statue of the Greek god Zeus at Olympia is evidence of the high level of importance the Greeks placed on their pantheon of gods.

their behavior was judged by the gods; in others, that perspective was totally absent. Some cultures went to extreme lengths to placate and honor their gods, including killing animals and humans as sacrifices, while others simply offered food, prayers, flowers, incense, clothing, or nothing at all. Some built huge and elaborate temples, statues, and monuments to honor and/or house their gods; others crafted small clay or straw figurines as representations of their deities. In some cultures the gods were central to daily life, in others peripheral.

The records of ancient mythologies vary in completeness and reliability. Since most extinct civilizations did not write down information about their gods during the time they were worshiped, learning about them often involves piecing stories together from various later sources, including ones from other cultures, which may be biased. Historians prize images of deities inscribed on objects like pottery and temple walls, or carved as statues in the gods' likeness. These fragments give researchers clues to past beliefs and value systems. And by learning more about the amazing assortment of gods and goddesses in ancient cultures, modern-day people learn more about themselves and the origins of their own beliefs.

Egyptian Deities: The Duality of Nature

Chapter One

By 2000 B.C., Egyptian scribes had begun writing down myths about their deities in picture-writing called hieroglyphics. The exploits of the gods and goddesses were carved on tomb and temple walls all over Egypt, but not until the mid-1800s were scholars able to decipher the hieroglyphics. Before that, the only known Egyptian myth was the story of the god Osiris, written in the first century B.C. by the Greco-Roman historian Plutarch. This text—the only fully recorded Egyptian myth that has survived—still serves as the foundation for understanding the roles the gods and goddesses played in ancient Egyptian society.

A Pantheon Emerges

When the earliest tribes first settled the area beside the fertile Nile River, they brought with them the idea that every aspect of life, including the forces of nature and nature itself, was controlled by supernatural beings.

Little was known about Egyptian mythology until scholars were able to decipher hieroglyphics in the 1800s.

They thought of these beings as vague, powerful forces rather than figures with human form. However, when the first pharaoh united the various towns of Egypt around 3000 B.C., a more accessible and solidified group of nine major gods and goddesses (known as the Ennead) began to emerge. The deities took on recognizable forms—either humanistic, animalistic, or both—along with a clear role in either the creation or function of the world.

The basic characteristics of the gods developed from the Egyptians' notion of duality. According to historian Mary Barnett, the physical location of the ancient Egyptian civilization—wedged between the lush Nile River Valley and the unforgiving desert—helps explain the inhabitants' belief in the dual nature of life: "The power of the sun could be both beneficial and life-threatening, and the absence of the sun during the dark and cold desert nights was a contrasting feature of the environment. Day and night, east and west, desert and river, flood and drought, sowing and harvest, death and rebirth, good and evil—they were perhaps more intensely felt in the Nile valley than they were elsewhere."[3] To the ancient Egyptians, their gods and goddesses represented various aspects of these contrasts, depicting the dual nature of the external natural world, the human life cycle, and human behavior.

Ra and Apep: Day and Night

The Egyptians considered the sun the life-giving force of the universe, and Ra, the sun god, was therefore their most powerful deity. In keeping with his high position, Ra (also known as Re) was believed as well to be the creator-god who ushered the other primary gods and goddesses into being and watched over them. In that role he was referred to as Atum-Ra or Ra-Atum. Ra's greatest responsibility, however, was to ensure that day turned into night, and night back into day. For without that, life could not continue.

The story of how Ra completed his task has been told in two different ways. In one version Ra actually personified the sun, which was considered to be either his body or his eye. As the sun traveled its daily path across the sky, do did Ra travel the length of

The sun god Ra crosses the heavens in this depiction of an ancient Egyptian myth that explains how day turns to night.

The Egyptian Book of the Dead

The gods played as important a role in Egyptians' deaths as they did in their lives. When individuals died, their graves would likely be decorated with symbols of various deities whose job it was to protect the soul as it waited to be judged by Osiris in the Hall of Two Truths. The Egyptians hoped they would be judged worthy of a happy afterlife, and they hoped the gods would assist them. A papyrus reproduction of what the ancient Egyptians called *The Book of Going Forth by Day* (now called *The Egyptian Book of the Dead,* translated here by Raymond Faulkner) was often buried in the coffins. With detailed illustrations and hieroglyphics, the book described the journey the soul would take on its way to meet Osiris. The Egyptians hoped the text would help them make a smoother transition to the afterlife. The book begins:

Here begin the chapters of going out into the day,
the praises and recitations for going to and fro in the
Gods' Domain which are beneficial in the beautiful
West, and which are to be spoken on the day of
burial and of going in after coming out.

Hail, O ye who make perfect souls to enter into the House of Osiris, make ye the well-instructed soul of the Osiris the scribe Ani, whose word is true, to enter in and to be with you in the House of Osiris. Let him hear even as ye hear; let him have sight even as ye have sight; let him stand up even as ye stand up; let him take his seat even as ye take your seats.

his life. He was born each day at dawn, then grew older as the day progressed. He was a child in the morning, a full-grown man at noon, an old man at sunset, and by nightfall he was dead, only to be reborn the following dawn. With his death came the dark of night, with his rebirth the sunrise.

In the most widely related story of how day turns to night, Ra played a much more active role. In ancient times, Egypt was divided into twelve regions. Ra's job was to cross the heavens during the day in a boat called Mandjet, and spend equal time (one hour) surveying each of the twelve regions. The Egyptians believed that as an all-seeing god, Ra was able to pass judgment over them as he passed overhead. Thus people were constrained to behave well, lest they anger or upset a god as important as Ra. As dusk fell, Ra took on the form of a ram's head and switched to his night ship, the Mesektet, which would take him into the underworld. For the next twelve hours he sailed through the land of the dead, passing through twelve caverns filled with monsters, and giving solace to the souls resting there.

Ra's biggest threat in the underworld was a gigantic serpent named Apep, who embodied evil, chaos, and darkness. He had become Ra's archenemy, and his one goal was to stop Ra's journey before dawn. Every night Apep would attack Ra's ship and the two would battle. With help from his fellow gods (including the usually antagonistic Seth), Ra always won the fight and emerged from the underworld to again traverse the heavens and bring daylight to the land. For the Egyptians, the battle of light versus dark, day versus night, would play out for eternity through the battles of Ra and Apep. For without this battle, there could be no day, no night, and no life on earth.

Pairings of Nature: Shu and Tefnut, Geb and Nut

The idea of duality is reflected in the ancient Egyptians' creation myth. In the beginning, all that existed was an ocean of chaos called Nun from which sprung Atum-Ra, the creator god. Atum-Ra then created two children who were really two halves of one whole: Shu, the god of air and sunlight, and Tefnut, the goddess of moisture and the moon. One day the pair disappeared, leaving their father devastated. He searched for them with his all-seeing eye, and when they were finally returned to him, Atum-Ra's tears of joy created mankind. Due to the power of Ra's sight, the Eye of Ra (called the Wadjet) became an important Egyptian symbol

The Wadjet, or Eye of Ra, is an important Egyptian symbol that is seen often in Egyptian artwork. It is believed to protect Egyptians from evil.

believed to ward off evil. Carved and painted on coffins and temple walls and fashioned into jewelry, the symbol was believed to protect Egyptians from harm.

With the birth of Shu and Tefnut, there was now air and moisture, but nothing else. So the pair gave birth to Geb, the god of earth, and Nut, the goddess of the sky and heavens. In keeping with their integral relationship to each other, Geb and Nut were born stuck together. Their father, Shu, had to pry them apart by pulling on Nut's body while her hands and feet remained firmly planted on the ground. In that position, they encompassed all the world forever.

Once the external elements of the world were in place, Geb and Nut created the four deities whose story laid the foundation for the Egyptian belief in the afterlife—Osiris, Isis, Nephthys, and Seth.

Osiris: Life and Death

The myth of Osiris is noteworthy in that it represents not only one, but two dualities crucial to life in ancient Egypt—the annual death and renewal of the crops, and the death and afterlife of the people. It is also the only Egyptian myth historians have discovered intact. The intriguing story begins when Osiris's father, Geb, asks his son to take over as ruler of Egypt. With the help of his loving wife, the sky and fertility goddess Isis, Osiris eagerly made positive changes in Egyptian society. Together they civilized the people by abolishing the practice of cannibalism, taught them the tools of agriculture, and exposed them to knowledge and the alphabet. They even provided a temperate climate for crops to thrive. One day Osiris decided

his guidance was needed in the rest of the world, so he took off and left the capable Isis in charge. As queen of Egypt, Isis was much beloved, as much for her magical healing powers as for her kindness and dedication.

When Osiris later returned to Egypt, everyone welcomed him back except for his brother Seth, a wicked god. Jealous of Osiris's power and popularity, Seth devised a plan to take over as ruler. With cunning and expert craftsmanship, Seth constructed a chest that would fit Osiris's exact measurements. He then tricked Osiris into getting inside. Before Osiris could climb out, Seth slammed the lid shut and sealed it tight. He then threw it into the Nile, assuming the great god would suffocate before the chest was found. The chest eventually washed up on the shore and became entwined with the roots of a tree. Meanwhile, Isis was devastated by the loss of her husband and dutifully searched for him far and wide. She finally stumbled upon the tree, which had been made into a pillar for the local king's palace. Disguising herself as a nurse, she was hired by the queen to care for her new baby. This allowed her to be near the pillar while she figured out a plan. While caring for the baby, she decided to make him immortal by dipping him into the fire each night. When the queen saw this, Isis was forced to reveal her true self. The king took pity on her and agreed to let her have the pillar. Isis pulled out the chest and opened it, only to find Osiris long dead. She brought the chest back to Egypt with her and hid it in the marshes.

Before long, Seth learned of Isis's discovery and found the chest himself. He cut up Osiris's body into fourteen pieces and

Anubis preserves the body of Osiris while Osiris's wife Isis, in the form of a bird, is shown flying overhead.

scattered them around the country. To find the pieces, Isis enlisted the help of her sister Nephthys. Nephthys was Seth's wife, but she opposed his evil ways and was eager to help her sister. Together the two goddesses gathered the pieces of Osiris's body and molded him together again. Isis then turned herself into a bird and flapped around her husband's body, magically breathing life back into it. Osiris came back to life long enough to impregnate her with the god Horus. When Osiris expired again, Nephthys sent for her son Anubis, the jackal-headed god of embalming, to preserve the body. Anubis wrapped Osiris in cloths, making him the first mummy.

Osiris then began his new role as ruler of the underworld, but occasionally reappeared on Earth to guide his son Horus on his path toward avenging his death.

The life and death and rebirth of Osiris gave the Egyptians hope that they too would be reborn after they died. The concept of the afterlife permeated Egyptian culture: Egyptians believed that the story of Osiris paved the way for their own death experience, and that Osiris waited for them in the underworld to judge their souls. Following Anubis's example, they embalmed and mummified the bodies of important members of society and buried valuable objects with them, to be used in the afterlife. The priests whispered to the dead the details of their journey to the underworld where, with one simple test, Anubis would help Osiris oversee their fate.

Anubis, Toth, and Maat: Reward Versus Punishment

For the ancient Egyptians, the most important part of the afterlife experience was the moment their ultimate fate was decided. When they faced Osiris in his underworld Hall of Two Truths, only two outcomes were possible—reward or punishment—as measured by the god Anubis and the goddess Maat. Egyptian men and women lived their lives knowing they would one day be judged in light of their actions on Earth. As a result, people went to great lengths to encourage the priests to make offerings to the gods on their behalf. This included building temples and paying taxes to support the priests in their intricate daily rituals. The priests would first anoint an image of the god by putting sacred oil on it, and then they would offer the

Ancient Egyptian artwork portrays Osiris (far left) at the Hall of Two Truths, where a dead person's heart was weighed and his ultimate fate decided.

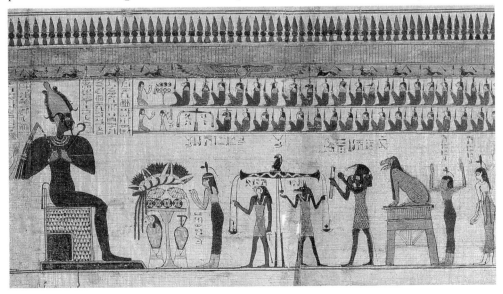

The Coffin Texts

As recorded by scholar R. T. Rundle Clark in his book *Myth and Symbol in Ancient Egypt*, Passage 148 in the ancient *Coffin Texts* allows the great god Horus to speak in his own words:

I am Horus, the great Falcon upon the ramparts of the house of him of the hidden name. My flight has reached the horizon. I have passed by the gods of Nut. I have gone further than the gods of old. Even the most ancient bird could not equal my very first flight. I have removed my place beyond the powers of Set [Seth], the foe of my father Osiris. No other god could do what I have done. I have brought the ways of eternity to the twilight of the morning. I am unique in my flight. My wrath will be turned against the enemy of my father Osiris and I will put him beneath my feet in my name of Red Cloak.

image food, incense, and even clothing. By doing this, they were ensuring the world behaved as it should—that the sun rose, the crops flourished, the people and land were fertile, and the journeys of the dead were successful. When people died, however, their fate rested only in their hands as the god Anubis guided them through the underworld.

Once the recently deceased reached the Hall of Two Truths, they would meet Maat, the goddess of truth and justice, and Toth, the god of wisdom and learning. Maat would pluck the single ostrich feather (representing justice) from her headdress and lay it on one side of a scale. Anubis would then place the dead person's heart on the other side of the scale. If the scale was evenly balanced, the person was blessed with a peaceful afterlife in the underworld. If the heart was too heavy and weighed down the scale, a monster named Ammut stood ready to devour the unfortunate individual.

Faced with one of these two fates in the afterlife, Egyptians were consumed by the internal struggle between good and evil. They allowed two gods—Horus and Seth—to personify this constant conflict.

Horus and Seth: Good Versus Evil

According to the myth of Osiris, the god Seth represented all that was immoral, corrupt, envious, and untrustworthy in the world. Following the duality of the mythology, Seth's antithesis was the ancient Egyptians' righteous hero. That hero was Horus, the falcon-headed son of Isis and the slain Osiris. Together, the story of Horus and Seth portrays the ongoing battle between good and evil, and teaches that goodness will triumph in the end.

In the legend, Horus's mother Isis had raised him in secret, hoping to keep her brother Seth from learning of the boy's existence. Seth ruled Egypt when Osiris died, but as Osiris's son, the throne rightly belonged to Horus. Isis knew, however, Seth would not relinquish his power without a fight. When Seth eventually did find out about Horus, he attacked the boy in the form of many poisonous creatures. Each time Horus's strength allowed him to survive the attacks and continue training so that he could one day defeat his uncle. Horus was often visited by the spirit of his dead father, who helped teach him the ways of war. When he was ready, Horus set out to find Seth. The two gods battled for three full days and nights until Horus defeated his foe. Isis was left to deal with the captured Seth, but he tricked her into letting him go. Horus caught up with him again and, though his own eye was ripped out in the process, managed to defeat Seth for good. The gods restored Horus's eye and named him ruler of Egypt. Seth was banished to the sea, where he became the god of storms.

The victorious Horus became one of the most important and celebrated gods in Egypt. He embodied righteousness, and every king of Egypt was considered an incarnation of him. To the ancient Egyptians, the strength of character that Horus embodied gave them insight into the nature of goodness, which by exalting him they hoped to achieve themselves. Similarly, the

The god Horus was revered by the ancient Egyptians, who considered him the embodiment of righteousness.

story of Seth served as a warning that evil would lead only to destruction in the end.

The Egyptian gods and goddesses were worshiped longer than any other in recorded history—at least thirty-five hundred years. In the fourth century A.D., the Roman emperor Theodosius decreed that the Egyptian reli-gion be brought to an end. He ordered the destruction of the temples and replaced them with Roman ones. A few centuries later, the influence of the Islamic religion left no more room for the worship of the ancient deities who remain so firmly at the heart of Egypt's history.

Hindu Deities: 333 Million Manifestations of Divinity

With approximately 900 million followers, Hinduism is the third-largest religion in the world today. It is also the world's most enduring religion, having emerged in India at least thirty-five hundred years ago. Many argue that Hinduism should be considered a way of life, a moral code, and a path to universal oneness, not a religion. Yet Hinduism has a mythology, and today the huge pantheon of Hindu gods and goddesses are still worshiped in public temples and private homes with the devotion with which they were revered in ancient times.

At 333 million, the number of deities in the world's only living mythology is staggering. The philosophical concepts behind Hinduism are equally overwhelming in their complexity and contradictory nature. The basic ideology behind Hindu gods and goddesses, however, is rather straightforward. Hindus believe in one Supreme Being who is composed of three main gods. These gods, known as the Supreme Triad, each have a primary consort or "wife" who complements or enhances traits they themselves possess or lack. Both the gods of the Triad and goddess wives have many offshoots of themselves—different incarnations and manifestations—which accounts for the countless number of deities. The unity of the gods springs from the Hindu outlook on life, which three scholars of Hinduism define as, "everything in the universe, every creature and plant, is a manifestation of Brahman [the Ultimate Reality] and thus contains an element of the divine.

The many gods reflect different aspects of the divine unity."[4] It is through their myths that the gods are able to demonstrate their particular traits, strengths, and weaknesses.

Ancient Tales, Vital Texts

The histories of the Hindu gods are based on a few sacred ancient texts, the oldest being the Vedas, which were composed by the Aryan people who settled in the Indus Valley around 2000 B.C. The Vedas existed in oral form as recently as 1500 B.C., but were not recorded in Sanskrit until much later. The first and most important Veda is the Rig-Veda, a collection of 1,028 hymns to the gods. Together with the Yajur-Veda, the Sama-Veda, and the Atharva-Veda, the series of sacred hymns honored the thirty-three gods of the Aryans and taught the people how to worship them.

As the Hindu gods were beginning to supplant the earlier Vedic gods (those written about in the Vedas), two epic Hindu poems, together known as the *Epics*, were written. The *Ramayana* is an account of the Hindu myths, and the *Mahabharata*, which includes a long section called the Bhagavad Gita (meaning "Song of the Lord"), contains the basic tenets of Hinduism. Together with the Puranas, a collection of sacred texts containing ancient beliefs, myths, and rituals, these accounts of the Hindu gods and goddesses and the creation of the universe serve as the foundation of much of Hindu spirituality and philosophy.

Indra, Vedic god of the sky, war, and fertility, and ruler of all other gods.

The Old Gods and the Vedic Trinity

It is important to recognize that the Vedic gods were predecessors of the Hindu gods; to understand the Hindu Triad, therefore, one must first examine the Vedic Triad. Three gods form the triad of the supreme ancient gods of the Vedics.

Indra, the sky god, is the chief god discussed in the Rig-Veda. He is the god of war and fertility and considered king of all the gods. He is selfish, proud, strong, and aggressive. He controls thunder and lightning, and can make rain. Indra once became jealous of the attention lavished on the virtuous son of a powerful Brahman (upper-class citizen). He tried to entice the boy to surrender his life of holiness, and when the boy remained virtuous, he sent down a bolt of lightning to kill him. Enraged, the boy's father conjured up a huge, powerful demon named Vritra, who swallowed Indra. Rescued by the other gods, Indra had to promise he would never attack Vritra in the daytime or at night, with any weapon dry or wet, or with any weapon made from stone, wood, or iron. Refusing to give up, Indra met Vritra at the seashore at dusk. He took a column of foam

A statue of Agni, the fire god, whose two heads personify the two types of fire—domestic and sacrificial.

from the sea and hurled it at the demon, killing him instantly. He did not break his pledge, for dusk was neither day nor night, and the foam was neither wet nor dry.

The second god in the triad is Agni, the fire god. He can grant immortality and purge the sins of the dead. He is often depicted with his red face smeared with the butter of sacrificial offerings. As the fire god, he is often depicted with two heads to personify the two types of fire—domestic and sacrificial. He has control over lightning, and created the columns of smoke that hold up the sky. He is considered a kind and generous

god, and is invoked to gain food, prosperity, and worldly goods. Together with Indra, Agni is given offerings of rice every autumn and barley every spring in thanks for saving the crops from the wrath of demons.

Completing the Vedic Triad is Surya, the sun god. Worshipers will perform daring feats with fire in the hope that Surya will recognize their devotion and grant them good fortune. They then bring offerings of food to the nearest body of water. Surya once had a wife named Sanjna, who found the glow that surrounded her husband too bright to bear. She decided to leave him, and

Physical Attributes of Major Hindu Deities

Since the Hindu deities are considered alive and well and able to visit Earth, Hindus are taught to recognize each deity by his or her physical appearance. Much emphasis is placed on the color of a deity's skin and the objects a deity holds and is surrounded by. Even specific facial expressions and body language are associated with various qualities of individual deities. Some of the more recognizable are:

Agni: Wild black hair, seven flaming tongues, sharp golden teeth, three arms, seven legs, and black eyes.

Brahma: Dresses in white, riding a swan or peacock or sitting on a lotus blossom.

Sarasvati: Usually pictured in white clothes on a white lotus playing a lute.

Vishnu: Dark blue skin, dresses in yellow with many jewels, often pictured carrying a lotus blossom in one hand, a golden mace in another, a discus in the third, and a conch shell in the fourth.

Lakshmi: Depicted holding gold coins, wearing red clothes with a golden lining and standing on a lotus next to small elephants.

Shiva: His light skin has a blue cast to it, with his throat the darkest blue. He has four arms and a third eye in the middle of his forehead; wears a snake wrapped around his neck, a tiger skin over his shoulders, and carries a trident.

Ganesha: A pot-bellied man with an elephant head and one tusk, often pictured with a mouse.

Kali: Dark black skin, four arms, earrings of corpses, a necklace of skulls, a belt of severed hands, wild hair, a blood-smeared face, red eyes, fangs, and a protruding tongue.

Durga: A weapon in each of her ten hands, she rides a powerful tiger or lion.

Shaya, the goddess of shade, took her place. When Surya eventually realized what had happened, he came up with a solution that benefited everyone. He allowed his father-in-law to shave off one-eighth of his brightness so that Sanjna could again be near him. The extra pieces fell to earth, where they turned into weapons for his fellow gods.

Although some of their characteristics were taken on by later Hindu gods, the three gods in the Vedic Triad continue to be respected in their own right as representations of the forces of nature and granters of fertility.

The Supreme Hindu Triad

The three most important Hindu gods—again, aspects of the one Supreme God—are Brahma, Vishnu, and Shiva. Together, they personify the three phases of life—creation, preservation, and death—a cycle of reincarnation that Hindus believe is continually repeated. It is not only people who are constantly reborn; the whole world is created, thrives, dies, and is then reborn. The three primary gods personify these three stages of life, but they do not do so alone. Each is paired with a goddess who is referred to as an aspect of Devi, the female manifestation of the triad.

Brahma, Sarasvati, and Creation

Brahma is the father of gods and men, creator of the universe, and guardian of the Vedas. As the living representation of Brahman, he is the essence of all things. According to myth, he was born in one of two ways, either growing from a lotus in the navel of the god Vishnu or emerging from a golden egg afloat in the cosmic waters.

Brahma is believed to have manifested into a thousand-headed primordial being named Purusha (also called "the cosmic man") in order to create the universe. As Purusha, he allowed himself to be cut into many pieces. Out of his mouth came the other gods, while his eyes became the sun, his head the sky, and his feet the earth.

Brahma's wife Sarasvati, a beautiful river goddess and the goddess of speech, knowledge, and wisdom, emerged from his side. As she modestly moved away, he turned toward her. With each movement of the goddess, Brahma grew another face so he could see her from that angle. Eventually Sarasvati flew up into the sky to escape his advances, but Brahma grew a fifth face on top of his head and he found her. Together they gave birth to the first race of people. Soon after, Brahma's fifth face was destroyed in a fight with the god Shiva for lusting after one of his wives. Brahma's status gradually declined as the other two gods of the triad surged in popularity, leaving him without a following.

The multi-headed Hindu god Brahma is regarded as the creator of the universe and the essence of all things.

Vishnu, Lakshmi, and Krishna

The second god in the Hindu Triad is Vishnu, the preserver of life, the

The Ten Avatars of Vishnu

The god Vishnu preferred to stay out of human affairs. Instead, he incarnated himself in different forms and sent these incarnations (called avatars) to Earth in his place. These are the ten avatars of Vishnu:

Matsya: a fish who saved the first man from the great flood.

Varaha: a boar who rescued the earth from demons who had dragged it to the bottom of the ocean.

Kurma: A turtle who supported the mountain that was used to churn the Ocean of Milk in order to grant immortality to the gods.

Narasimha: A half man/half lion who slew an otherwise invincible demon who could not be killed by any regular god or beast.

Vamana: A dwarf who saved the world by growing to superhuman size and covering the world in three steps, freeing it from the demon Bali.

Parasurama: Known as "Rama with an ax," this avatar freed the earth from oppression and safeguarded the caste system.

A sculpture of the Hindu god Vishnu features multiple heads representing his ten incarnations.

Prince Rama: The most virtuous hero in Indian mythology, and the focus of the Ramayana.

Krishna: Sent to rid the world of demons, he became a god in his own right.

Buddha: Siddhartha Gautama founded Buddhism, a religious philosophy that became more popular outside India than within.

Kalkin: This warrior avatar has not been sent to Earth yet. When it does, it will be in the form of either a white horse, a horse-headed man, or a man riding a white horse brandishing a flaming sword. He will usher in a new age.

god of love who balances good and evil in the world. Gentle, compassionate, and much beloved, he tries to only use nonviolent means to protect humanity and avert disaster. Lakshmi, the goddess of beauty, good fortune, and both inner and outer prosperity, is his wife. She is one of the most popular Hindu goddesses and is worshiped in many homes at small shrines.

When the world is in trouble, Vishnu incarnates himself into an avatar (physical manifestation of himself) and descends to Earth from his heavenly realm to help humanity. In total, he has created nine different avatars, and legend has it that his tenth and last avatar will usher in a new cycle of creation. The eighth avatar of Vishnu, Krishna, is considered a god in his own right.

Krishna was identified as an avatar of Vishnu when, as a child, he opened his mouth wide and his mother saw all of the universe inside. Krishna grew up into a playful and popular young man who used his extraordinary strength to help mankind. His divine power was challenged once by the Vedic god Indra. Krishna had advised the people to stop offering sacrifices to Indra, and in retaliation Indra sent down a torrential downpour to punish the people who listened to Krishna's advice. To protect the people and their cattle, Krishna lifted Mount Govardhana with a single finger and used it as an umbrella over their heads.

Besides being known for his great strength, Krishna has a leading role in the Bhagavad Gita, when he explains the connection of humanity with the divine to a surprised warrior named Arjuna. He claims Vishnu is the most important god of all, an assertion that devoted followers of Shiva continue to dispute.

Shiva, Parvati, and Ganesha

The god with the widest following is Shiva, or Siva, the god of destruction and of mercy, the lord of the dance, the god of sexual power, yoga, and meditation. Shiva's worshipers often try to follow his ascetic ways, based on austerity and self-denial. Shiva is considered the oldest god in India, not only

A bronze statue of Shiva, the most popular and powerful god in the Hindu Triad.

Krishna Speaks: The Bhagavad Gita

In chapter 3, verses 6 through 12 of the Bhagavad Gita (translated here by Jean Mascaro) the Lord Krishna (an avatar of the god Vishnu) acts as a guide for the warrior Prince Arjuna and teaches him some basic tenets of Hinduism:

6. He who withdraws himself from actions, but ponders on their pleasures in his heart, he is under a delusion and is a false follower of the Path.

7. But great is the man who, free from attachments, and with a mind ruling its powers in harmony, works on the path of Karma Yoga, the path of consecrated action.

8. Action is greater than inaction: perform therefore thy task in life. Even the life of the body could not be if there were no action.

9. The world is in the bonds of action, unless the action is consecration. Let thy actions then be pure, free from the bonds of desires.

10. Thus spoke the Lord of Creation when he made both man and sacrifice: By sacrifice thou shalt multiply and obtain all thy desires.

11. By sacrifice shalt thou honour the gods and the gods will then love thee. And thus in harmony with them shalt thou attain the supreme good.

12. For pleased with thy sacrifice, the gods will grant to thee the joy of all thy desires. Only a thief would enjoy their gifts and not offer them in sacrifice.

because he appeared in the Rig-Veda as a Vedic god named Rundra, but because Rundra himself was most likely based on an even older European god. Shiva proved his position as the most powerful god in the triad by besting Vishnu and Brahma. Shiva stuck a huge stone pillar into the cosmic waters and then disappeared. The other two tried to see who could find an end of the column first. Brahma flew up to try to find the top of the column while Vishnu flew downward into the water. For a thousand years they flew, only to return exhausted without reaching either end. At this point the column burst

open and Shiva appeared within. The others were forced to recognize that the column was really Shiva's life force, which proved greater than either of theirs.

Shiva demonstrated this power when he saved the world from being poisoned. At one time, the gods were weakened and agreed to join demons to create the Ocean of Milk, which would grant them all immortality. With the help of a great snake named Vasuki and a living mountain named Mandara, the gods churned the waters to create an immortality elixir. The force of the churning, however, caused the snake to emit a powerful venom that threatened to destroy the world. Shiva recognized the danger and swallowed the poison, thereby allowing the gods to gain their immortality while saving the people and animals of the earth.

The history of Shiva's home life is a bit more complicated than the tales of his amazing feats. His first wife, the goddess Sati, was very devoted to him. When her own father ignored Shiva at a feast, Sati was so ashamed

A statue of the pot-bellied elephant god Ganesha, god of success, wisdom, and beginnings.

that she threw herself into the fire. Luckily, she was reborn as the goddess Parvati, the aggressive daughter of the Himalayan mountains and goddess of fertility. Parvati tried for a long time to get Shiva's attention, including standing on one leg for a full year. But the god was too busy meditating to notice her. Finally the god Indra sent a god of love to shoot Shiva with an arrow to awaken him. When he finally saw Parvati he fell in love. Together they began the model holy family with the birth of their son Ganesha, an account of whose birth takes two significant forms.

In one version of the story, Parvati was lonely and wanted a child. She wiped off some sweat, added soap from her bath, and created Ganesha, the popular god of wisdom, success, and beginnings. Ganesha is very loyal to his mother and would not let Shiva into the room where she was bathing. Shiva was angry and chopped off Ganesha's head. Parvati was so upset that Shiva promised he would resurrect their son. He sent his attendants to find the first creature they came across, which happened to be an elephant. They cut off the elephant's head, and Shiva attached it to Ganesha's body and brought him back to life.

In the second version, Shiva created Ganesha for his wife out of a piece of her red gown. She was very happy until Shiva took the baby in his arms and the baby's head fell off. Shiva promised to fix him and sent his servant to find the perfect head. The servant came back with the head of an elephant belonging to the god Indra and the boy was revived. Regardless of his origin, Ganesha, who rides on the back of a rat, is pictured with a human body, four arms, a pot belly, and an elephant's head with one tusk missing. Supposedly he either wore down the tusk by inscribing all eleven thousand verses of the *Mahabharata,* or broke it off to hurl at a demon in the sky. As the remover of obstacles, Ganesha is invoked with red flowers and desserts before any new venture to ensure success. In fact, he is so popular that he is often worshiped before any of the three gods in the triad. Only one other deity outside of the triad receives such devotion; her name is Kali.

The Black Mother and the Bloodthirsty Goddess

Kali, known as the Black Mother, is the goddess of nature, destruction, and energy. Her image is frightening, and like that of Ganesha, the story of her birth varies. Some say that Shiva teased his wife Parvati about her dark skin, so she scraped her body until it became golden. It is that discarded layer of skin that became Kali. This story would also explain why Kali is referred to as a wife of Shiva. In another version of the story, Kali burst forth in anger from the forehead of the goddess Durga in the midst of a great battle against seemingly endless demons. Kali swallowed all the demons and saved

the world. She was so excited after the battle that she continued to rage around the world, stopping only when she realized she was killing her own husband Shiva by dancing atop his body.

Although Kali is associated with death and destruction, she is also honored for destroying bad things like ignorance and pain. She is credited with inventing Sanskrit, and brings comfort to those in fear by explaining that the next stage of life after destruction (death) is creation (birth). Goats are sometimes sacrificed to her, although today many Hindus offer cooked meats instead. A few hundred years ago a cult dedicated to her reportedly sacrificed humans in her name.

As one version of her creation demonstrates, Kali is often associated with Durga, a strong, bloodthirsty goddess who is also considered a wife of Shiva. Unlike Kali, however, Durga is often depicted as beautiful and serene as she combats evil. Born in the midst of a battle between the gods and a buffalo-demon named Mahishasura who could only be conquered by a woman, Durga was created from fire shooting out of the gods' mouths. Riding a lion and brandishing a weapon in each of her ten hands, she attacked the demon, who turned himself into a buffalo, a lion, a man, and an elephant before turning back into a buffalo. At one point, the demon fell in love with Durga and proposed marriage. Instead, Durga killed him. As a result, young women now offer Durga flowers, leaves, and fruit in the hopes of finding their mate. Due to Durga's triumph in battle, all the goddesses

The Secret Cult of Kali

The devotees of Kali accept that the world can be a violent place, and that by being closer to Kali they can transcend that which is good and evil. The belief that Kali needed blood sacrifices to continue the cycle of destruction and creation led to the formation of a murderous cult that terrorized India for nearly three hundred years. The cult called itself Thuggee, from the Hindi verb thagna, *which means "deceive" and from which the English word* thug *originated. The group, composed mostly of respected members of society leading a double life, killed innocent victims by strangling them with specially knotted cloths. What started out as sacrifice in the name of religious idolatry eventually became murder in the name of political idealism as the Thuggees rallied against British colonialism. Finally the Indian government joined forces with the British police and the activities of the Thuggees were stopped in 1837.*

An eighteenth-century portrayal of the goddess Kali, also known as the Black Mother.

A thirteenth-century depiction of the goddess Durga vanquishing the buffalo-demon Mahishasura.

grew in status until they were esteemed as highly as, if not higher than, the gods themselves.

A Living Mythology

As a reflection of the supreme esteem in which faithful Hindus hold their gods, 80 percent of Hindu children are named after a deity. More than ritual obligation, worship is an essential part of everyday life. Besides visiting temples, Hindus construct small shrines in their homes, which they visit at appointed times. Worship, called *puja*, includes lighting incense, ringing bells, lighting oil, chanting, and praying. On special occasions worship can include bringing flowers, food, or money to the temple or shrine. The various elements of Hindu worship, such as the type of flower or the kind of animal sacrificed, changes according to which deity is being praised on what occasion. It is important that Hindus are very familiar with the attributes each deity symbolizes so that they can worship properly.

Celtic Deities: A Love of High Adventure

Chapter Three

Never a truly unified society, the Celts consisted of tribes loosely grouped by similar customs, laws, and related languages. The first Celtic tribe is thought to have formed in central Europe by 800 B.C.; from that hub various splinter groups gradually spread across Europe. Although a small number reached Asia Minor, the majority of the Celtic tribes moved west. By 500 B.C. the Celts had a solid presence in Gaul (modern-day France), Britain (England, Scotland, and Wales), and Ireland; in these regions, until around 400 A.D., they left their mark on history.

For centuries Celtic myths were passed down orally, with priests called Druids having the sacred duty of keeping the tales alive. The only written sources of Celtic mythology were created long after the Celts had been Christianized by the Romans, a process that began in 54 B.C. when the Romans invaded Britain. As a result, much true Celtic lore has been lost and no one knows the extent and nature of the deities' influence on the culture. Nevertheless, the two written sources that do exist have helped scholars piece together some information about the Celtic gods and goddesses. From Ireland, twelfth-century sagas provide background on Celtic life in pre-Christian Ireland, with the *Mythological Cycle* focusing on the various mythic peoples to inhabit the island. Then in the fourteenth century, Welsh scholars wrote the *Mabinogion*, a collection of tales that related the exploits of the ancient Welsh gods and goddesses by disguising them as members of the royal houses of Wales. Taken together, these two sources reveal the differences and similarities between the Celtic gods of Ireland and Wales.

A tenth-century Celtic cross, carved with stories from the Bible. When the Celts adopted Christianity, much of their mythology was lost.

War, Nature, and Love Affairs

Because Celtic society was not centralized, Celtic gods and goddesses varied from tribe to tribe and between geographic areas. The tribes were linked, however, by a warrior mentality and an overall love of adventure and storytelling. As a result, the Celtic deities were imbued with high ideals, bravery, and the love of a good quest. According to historian Peter Berresford Ellis, "A happy spirit pervades even the [tragic myths]. There is an eternal spirit of optimism, a love

of nature, art, poetry, games, feasting, and heroic combat."[5]

The myths of the Celtic gods in Ireland had a different focus than those of Wales. Each deity of the Irish Celtic pantheon was given a role to play in either a heroic battle or in one of the four seasonal celebrations. In this fashion they served as both examples of bravery and strength for the Celtic people to emulate and protectors of the natural world. While the Irish Celtic deities were busy fighting invaders and being the focus of seasonal celebrations, the Welsh deities were entangled in messy familial problems and tumultuous love lives.

Irish Native Gods

According to a text known as *The Book of Invasions*—begun as early as the late sixth century A.D., and completed in the twelfth century— four waves of supernatural invaders landed in Ireland before the Celts arrived. In the absence of a creation myth explaining how the world came into being, the Celtic tribes of Ireland had myths about how their homeland was settled. When the first group of invaders arrived, the inhabitants of Ireland were known as the Fomori (or Fomhoire), which means "from the sea." They were believed to be ancient and evil gods, ancestors of all evil fairies, giants, and leprechauns, and the gods of night, death, and cold. Their bodies were misshapen, a condition that the Celts associated with an evil nature. Some were reported to have only one arm and one leg. Each wave of invading gods had to do battle with this powerful group.

The Four Invaders

The Partholonians arrived in Ireland from the west and were attacked by the mighty Fomori. The Partholonians won the battle and drove the Fomori into the northern seas. For a few hundred years the Partholonians lived in peace, clearing the land and creating lakes. Without warning, an outbreak of plague wiped out everyone except for a man named Tuan. He was the only Partholonian alive to greet the next band of invaders, the Nemedians.

The Nemedians also came from the west, and the Fomori returned from the seas to fight them. The Nemedians won a few battles, but eventually had to admit defeat. The evil gods then forced the Nemedians to hand over their children and their milk and corn. A small group managed to escape by boat to Greece before a terrible plague and a final battle with the Fomori finished off the rest of the Nemedian race.

A frieze of Celtic warriors from the second century B.C. *The Celts valued bravery, strength, and an adventurous spirit—traits that they assigned to their deities.*

Two hundred years later, a group called the Fir Bholg arrived and chose to worship the Fomori gods rather than fight with them. They divided the land into provinces and formed the first kingships. Their peaceful reign, however, was short-lived. The most powerful race of Celtic gods ever created was about to lay claim to the land.

The Tuatha de Danann, arriving in a clouded mist, were unlike any of their predecessors. Their name meant "the Children of Dana," Dana being the mother aspect of a triple goddess also composed of Anu, the virgin, and Badb, the crone. Dana was the greatest of the triple goddesses, a tradition in Celtic mythology based on their belief that the number 3 was sacred. The Tuatha de Danann came from the north and brought incredible magic powers and knowledge with them. They allowed the Fir Bholg to remain in Ireland and turned their attention to driving the Fomori from the land for good. The Celts chose to immortalize these powerful and heroic gods and goddesses through stories of their great deeds, and worship them at the dawn of each new season.

The Dagda Leads the Way

The Dagda, the chief of the Tuatha de Danann, was considered the father of all the people of Ireland. His name meant "the good god" and he played an integral part in leading the Irish Celts in and out of battles with

The Forest in the Water

In the twelfth century, Welsh scholars wrote four books known collectively as the *Mabinogion*. They tell the stories of the gods' exploits, their successes, and their failures. After many centuries, they were translated into English in the mid–nineteenth century by Lady Charlotte E. Guest. Here, in the tale entitled "Branwen the Daughter of Llyr," the goddess Branwen has been taken captive by Matholwch, king of Ireland, whom she had been forced to marry. Undaunted, Branwen reveals to her attendants that her brother is coming to rescue her.

Messengers then went unto Branwen. Lady, said they, what thinkest thou that this is? The men of the Island of the Mighty, who have come hither on hearing of my ill treatment and my woes. What is the forest that is seen upon the sea? asked they. The yards and the masts of ships, she answered. Alas, said they, what is the mountain that is seen by the side of the ships? Bendigeid Vran [Bran the Blessed], my brother, she replied, coming to shoal water; there is no ship that can contain him in it. What is the lofty ridge with the lake on each side thereof? On looking towards this island he is wroth, and his two eyes, one on each side of his nose, are the two lakes beside the ridge.

An engraving of Celtic warriors on horseback. The Irish Celts' most important deity, the Dagda, was revered for his role in leading the Celts into battles.

invading forces. He was wise, a master wizard, and a powerful fighter. In fact, the club he always carried was so large that he had to drag it behind him on wheels. With one end of the club he could kill his enemies, but the other end could restore them to life. Each of the fighting gods was given a special weapon or other item that would help assure his victory. In the case of the Dagda, he was given two items—his mighty club, and a magic "cauldron of plenty"—which supplied a never-ending flow of food to feed soldiers and whoever else was in need.

One day the Fomori took advantage of the Dagda's rapacious appetite and forced him to eat a huge bowl of porridge made from flour, milk, and animals. The Dagda used a giant ladle and ate the whole thing. He then mated with a Fomori woman in the hopes that their union would benefit their two tribes. Some sources claim the union was impossible because his stomach was too full from all the food. Regardless, the truce did not last long, and the Dagda needed help from two other great gods—Lugh and Nuada—to match his enemy's strength.

Lugh, Nuada, and Balor

One of the most beloved Celtic gods was Lugh, the many-skilled, fair-haired sun god referred to as Lugh of the Long Arm or "the

A statue of the god Nuada who, according to legend, lost a hand in battle and was asked to step down as leader of the Tuatha de Danann.

he returned to his homeland to join his people in battle against the Fomori.

At that time, the great god Nuada was the leader of the Tuatha de Danann. Nuada lost his hand in a battle with the Fir Bholg and had it replaced with a silver one. To the Celts, however, any physical deformity or disfigurement was a sign of weakness of character. As a result of his injury, the other gods asked Nuada to step down as leader. To keep his post, Nuada had a new arm of flesh and blood made and was given back his role as leader.

Once Lugh returned, however, Nuada graciously relinquished his position. He was convinced that the young man was the stronger, more skillful fighter. Both Lugh and Nuada had magical weapons that were supposed to make them invincible. Nuada's sword must not have been as powerful as Lugh's spear, however, because in the midst of a battle with the Fomori, Nuada was killed by Balor. Lugh, angered by Nuada's death, decided to make Balor pay for his actions. He knew Balor's weak spot, his one large eye, which was always covered with a thick eyelid. The evil eye had the power to kill anyone who saw it, so Lugh knew his timing had to be perfect. Just as Balor's guards were lifting his large eyelid so he could fight, Lugh used his slingshot and struck him in his half-open eye, killing him instantly and fulfilling the prophecy.

Shining One." Although related to the Fomori tribe through his grandfather Balor, Lugh was unaware of that fact for most of his life. When Balor's daughter Ethnea was pregnant with Lugh, Balor learned of a prophecy that his grandson would one day bring about his demise. To protect himself, Balor locked his pregnant daughter in a crystal tower. A few years after Lugh was born, he was rescued and raised far from his family. Lugh was not only remarkably strong and adept at fighting, he was also intelligent and skilled at games and music. When he was old enough to fight,

The Lord of the Beasts

Some Celtic gods do not figure neatly in any of the known myths, nor are traces of them found in all areas of Celtic habitation. The Celts in ancient Gaul (modern-day France) left few records of their mythology behind, but there is one name that historians keep digging up—Cernunnos, the Lord of the Beasts.

Cernunnos was a very ancient god who may even predate Celtic times. His worship was the strongest among Celtic tribes in central France. Cernunnos was "the Horned One," a god of fertility, prosperity, and the underworld. He is sometimes pictured as a man with ram-headed snakes for legs, and always with the long horns of a stag sticking out of the top of his head. Cernunnos is often surrounded by stags to indicate sexuality, serpents to symbolize death and fertility, horned bulls who appear often in Celtic myths as strong supernatural animals, and boars and other wild creatures associated with Cernunnos's role as god of the hunt. He is sometimes pictured feeding the animals, and may have been able to take on their forms.

An engraving depicts Cernunnos, Lord of the Beasts.

The End of the Tuatha de Danann

The mighty Fomori were finally defeated for good at the second battle of Magh Tuireadh and forced to take up residency under the oceans. Eventually newcomers, for the first time mortals, came into the land. This group, the forerunners of the Celtic people, were called the Milesians. An agreement was forged between the two groups which stated that the Milesians had the right to the upper domains of the earth while the Tuatha de Danann were relegated to the lower, underground realms. The once mighty and unbeatable gods were led under the earth by the Dagda. Although driven away, the deeds of the Tuatha de Danann were still invoked for centuries, especially at four seasonal festivals.

Samhain and the Fateful Affair

Each October 31/November 1 the Celts celebrated Samhain, the end of the harvest, whose name literally means "summer's end." According to Celtic scholar Charles Squire, that was when "the sun's power waned, and the strength of the gods of darkness, winter and the underworld grew great."[6] At this festival the Celts asked the gods to protect both the cattle who were reined in from the pastures and the seeds of the newly planted winter crops. To ensure the gods' cooperation during the upcoming cold, dark months, the priests sacrificed animals and humans.

It was believed that the veil between the real world and the Otherworld (the afterlife where gods and mortal souls dwelt) was thin on this night, and souls were able to leave and enter with ease. The patron god of the festival was the Dagda, who symbolized the bounty of the harvest, but the Morrigan was Samhain's patron goddess, who, in her incarnation as the emissary of death, represented the sleeping fields.

It was the Dagda's duty to mate with a goddess on Samhain to ensure a new god would be born after the winter, and the new year would arrive. He usually mated with the Morrigan, the powerful goddess of war and death, who together with the Dagda was responsible for turning the seasons. Like Dana, she was a triple goddess, embodying three stages of womanhood. At Samhain, she was depicted as the crone goddess to symbolize the dying year.

Each year on this night, the Morrigan would find the Dagda by the river with his magic cauldron and they would mate. One year, however, the Dagda chose to mate with a mother goddess named Boann instead of with the Morrigan. When the pair discovered Boann was pregnant, they used their magic to make the sun stand still for nine months so Boann's husband would not find out. The baby, named Oenghus (or Angus), the god of love, was then born on the same day he was conceived and no one was the wiser. Had she known of the affair, the Morrigan, who could take the form of a beautiful woman or a menacing crow, would not have been very forgiving.

The Morrigan was fierce, and liked to watch warriors on the battlefield although she often chose not to fight herself. She preferred to fly overhead as a crow or a raven to scare the enemies of the Tuatha de Danann by signaling their death. She had often protected Lugh's son, the half-mortal hero Cuchulainn, but turned on him when he didn't recognize her and refused her advances of love. When he died in battle she landed on one of his shoulders in the form of a crow and watched as his body was torn apart.

Exactly three months after the festival of Samhain, the Celts were ready to say goodbye to winter and to welcome the coming spring. For that event they chose to honor the goddess Brighid.

The Feast of Brighid

After three cold, dark months gathered around the fire, the Celts were ready for the end of winter. To usher in spring, a feast day was held in the beginning of February called Imbolc, which literally means "ewe's milk"

This ancient bronze head is believed to depict the Celtic goddess Brighid, who later became a patron saint of Ireland.

because that was the time of year the sheep's milk would start to flow in preparation for birthing lambs. The festival of light was celebrated in honor of the goddess Brighid (also called Brigid or Brigit), the daughter of the mother goddess Dana and the father god, the Dagda. Like Dana and the Morrigan, Brighid was a triple goddess. One aspect of her was the patron of craftsmen and metalworkers; one was the goddess of poetry, wisdom, and learning; and the third was a healing, fire, and fertility goddess. Brighid was an ideal patron goddess for Imbolc, since the people had

spent the winter protected by the warm fires in their hearths, and they were now ready to thank the fire goddess for renewing the fires of life after the dark months. On Imbolc, candles were lit in Brighid's name as a sign that the sunlight hours would soon lengthen and with warmth would come a rebirth of the land. Offerings of butter and bread were left on windowsills and fires were kept burning all day in hopes that Brighid would soon bring the spring.

Brighid was the wife of Bres, the god of agriculture, who led the Tuatha de Danann for a while when Nuada injured his hand. Brighid was in charge of tending the flocks because she was capable of feeding both animals and people without running out of food. She lived on long after the Celtics were Christianized. With a slight name change, she became known as one of the patron saints of Ireland, St. Brigit or St. Bride, who supposedly died in 523 A.D. She was so beloved in Ireland that after her death she was placed in the same tomb as St. Patrick. A perpetual flame was lit in her honor that was dutifully tended by nuns in Kildare, Ireland, for seven hundred years.

Belanus and His Fire

The sun god Belanus was celebrated at the festival of Beltaine, which means "fire of Bel." It was a celebration of new life and birth, a welcoming of summer. Just as Samhain was

An illustration of a story from Celtic folklore portrays a woman visiting with a Druid priest. The Druids were responsible for passing down the Celtic myths.

a time to bring in the herd, Beltaine was a time to send the animals back to the fields for grazing. With much to celebrate in nature's awakening, the day was merry and joyous. Fires were extinguished on the eve of Beltaine and the village Druids created one large bonfire from different types of wood at sunrise. Because the gods were believed to live in them, trees, especially oaks and yews, were sacred. In fact, the word *Druid* has been translated as "wise man of the oaks." Each home hearth was then relit with kindling from the Druids' flame to bring blessings of good fortune to the home. The lighting of the great bonfires symbolized Belanus bringing his light to Earth. Beltaine was also the day that the mother goddess annually conceived the sun god so that he could be reborn the following December in time for the winter solstice (the shortest day of the year).

Besides Belanus, many other Celtic deities from both Ireland and Wales are associated with Beltaine. The first mythical invaders, the Partholonians, arrived on May 1, and it was on that same day a few hundred years later that the plague arrived to wipe them out. The mighty Tuatha de Danann also arrived on Beltaine, and it was on Beltaine that they were pushed underground by the Milesians.

A Young Welsh God Goes Missing

It was also on Beltaine that Pryderi, one of the central figures of Welsh mythology, was returned to his parents, Rhiannon and Pwyll, after having been kidnapped as an infant. Pwyll, the god of the underworld, was one of two central deities in the Welsh pantheon. His wife, Rhiannon, a fertility goddess whose singing birds could wake the dead, was the other. Their story began as a love story and ended as a tale of moral fortitude.

Pwyll first spied Rhiannon mounted on a beautiful white horse and knew he must marry her. She agreed, though she was betrothed to a man named Gwawl. For her rejection, Gwawl cursed her, which left her barren for many years. When she finally gave birth to a son named Pryderi, the boy soon mysteriously disappeared. To avoid drawing blame, Rhiannon's servants smeared the goddess's face with blood while she was sleeping, and when she awoke they claimed she had eaten her baby. Pwyll believed the servants and was furious at his wife's deed. He forced Rhiannon to sit at the entrance of the castle and tell everyone who passed what had happened. Rhiannon bore her great misfortune with dignity and patience, never allowing herself to crumble. Finally Pryderi was found on Beltaine. He was returned to his family and all was forgiven. Pryderi was later featured in all four tales of the *Mabinogion*. After Pwyll died, Rhiannon married Manawyddan, a gentle god of fertility and crafts. Manawyddan saved his whole family when Rhiannon's old suitor Gwawl tried to kill them all again.

The family of Pwyll, Rhiannon, and Pryderi was not the only dysfunctional one in the Welsh Celtic tales. More often than not, the course of true love was torture, and parents and their children did not always get along.

A Tangled Web

Celtic gods from Wales fell into two main groups, the Children of Llyr and the Children of Don (the Welsh counterpart to the Irish goddess Dana). Llyr (or Lir) himself is hardly mentioned in Welsh mythology. He was a sea god, and the likely inspiration for Shakespeare's tragedy *King Lear*. He was the father of Manawyddan, Bran the Blessed, and their sister Branwen.

Bran the Blessed was a unique character. He was so huge that he could not fit in any boat and had to walk in the sea alongside his fleet. His fate was tied to that of his sister Branwen's. One day the Irish king Matholwch came to Wales and asked Bran for his sister's hand in marriage. Bran agreed, but did not consult the other members of the family. Their half brother Efnisien was angry and cut off the tails, lips, and ears of Matholwch's horses. Furious, Matholwch demanded compensation. To appease him, Bran gave him a very precious gift—a magic cauldron that could bring back the dead. When Bran later learned that Matholwch was mistreating Branwen by making her work in the kitchen even though she had borne a son (named Gwern), he immediately headed to Ireland with a fleet of soldiers. Matholwch planned an ambush, but Efnisien discovered the plot and killed the soldiers in their hiding places. The Irish had the upper hand in the ensuing battle, however, because the soldiers used the magic cauldron to revive themselves after they died. The baby Gwern was thrown into the fire and Bran himself was killed in the battle by a poisoned arrow. He instructed his men to sever his head and return it to England where it would guard against invaders from the east. Even once it was detached from his body, Bran's head was still able to talk and eat. Meanwhile, Branwen was so distraught after the battle that she soon died of a broken heart.

Arianrod and the Children of Don

A very different story of love and motherhood is the tale of the goddess Arianrod and her son Lleu. Arianrod was the daughter of the god Belanus and the goddess Don (leader of the Children of Don). She was the goddess of fertility and reincarnation whose boat carried dead warriors to their resting place. The story of how Arianrod became a mother has survived in two versions. In one tale, when still a maiden, she stepped over the body of her uncle, the god Math, and instantly gave birth to the hero god Lleu (or Llew) and Dylan, a sea god. Her brother, the god Gwydion, who had great magical powers, helped raise the boys. In the other version, her sons were actually fathered by Gwydion. As soon as Dylan was born, the infant immediately went to the sea and started swimming. He was later mistakenly killed by his uncle Govannon and his sad death was mourned by the crashing waves on the shores of all the Celtic lands.

Arianrod's son Lleu was the strongest of the Children of Don, and was invested with many of the same powers as the Irish god Lugh. The two gods led very different lives, however. Whether out of jealousy or a lust for power, Arianrod set out to make her son's life very difficult. She put a series of curses on him, including forbidding him a name until

The Last Invaders

The Conquest of the Sons of Mil is an important section of the Irish *Leabhar Gabh`ala: The Book of Conquests of Ireland* (known simply as *The Book of Invasions* and translated here by R. A. Stewart Macalister). The Sons of Mil drove the gods away, and became the ancestors of the Irish people:

The sons of Mil advanced to a landing in Inber Stainge. The Tuatha De Danann did not allow them to come to the land there, for they had not held parley with them. By their druidry they caused it to appear to the sons of Mil that the region was no country or island, territory or land at all, in front of them. They encircled Ireland three times, till at last they took the harbor at Inber Scene; a Thursday as regards the day of the week, on the day before the first of May, the seventeenth day of the moon; the Year of the World 3500. . . .

When the sons of Mil reached their landing-place they made no delay until they reached Sliab Mis; and the battle of Sliab Mis was fought between them and the Tuatha De Danann, and the victory was with the sons of Mil. Many of the Tuatha De Danann were killed in that battle. When the Tuatha De Danann were crushed and expelled in the battles that were fought between them, the sons of Mil took the lordship of Ireland.

she named him, forbidding him weapons unless she armed him, and forbidding him from marrying a human woman. Fortunately, Gwydion watched over him and tricked Arianrod into giving the boy weapons. When it came time for him to marry, Gwydion and Math magically created a woman out of flowers named Blodeuedd. Lleu fell in love and married her, only to have her betray him and run away with another man. Blodeuedd had tricked him into revealing how he could be killed, leaving Lleu no choice but to transform himself into an eagle. Gwydion eventually found Lleu, and restored him to human form. Gwydion knew what it was like to be made into an animal, because he himself had once been turned into a stag, a wild sow, and a wolf as punishment for betraying his uncle Math in his youth. Thus the strongest of the gods survived his lost love.

Dancing at Lughnasa

Lleu shared many traits of the Irish god Lugh, the sun god who was honored each summer at Lughnasa. Lughnasa was a harvest festival that marked the end of the growing season and the start of the fall harvest. As the summer lengthened and the days got shorter, the Celts felt that Lugh was losing his strength. They danced for him in hopes of a good harvest ahead. Lugh enjoyed the celebration and founded a tradition of holding annual games of strength and skill on that day to commemorate his

Bagpipe players in kilts perform in Scotland. Kilts and bagpipes are Celtic cultural traditions that have been retained by the Scots.

foster mother Tailtu, who had taken him in after he was rescued from Balor's tower. The holiday celebrated the alliance between the sun and the earth and commemorated Lugh's continual rebirth.

Due in part to its geographical isolation, the Roman presence in Ireland was minimal. This meant that the Irish were able to keep Celtic culture alive to a greater degree than the rest of Britain. Though Christianity eventually took over, some of the old traditions and gods are still honored in local festivals, and Gaelic, the modern form of a Celtic dialect, is one of the official languages of Ireland. Scotland has retained a strong tradition of clans and other Celtic cultural tokens like bagpipes and kilts. Even England has not completely abandoned its Celtic roots and still celebrates the glory of King Arthur and Camelot, even though any real King Arthur would likely have lived long after the Celtic civilization. Shrines, sacred sites, and sacrificial wells dot the Irish and British countryside, a standing reminder of the devotion with which the Celts served their gods.

Greek Deities: The Extremes of Human Emotion

Chapter Four

Ancient Greek mythology influenced every Western culture in existence today. The word *mythology*, meaning "an imaginative tale," was coined by the Greek philosopher Plato from the Greek word *mythos*. The Greek civilization began to thrive around 1500 B.C., after waves of settlers congregated on the mainland of the Greek peninsula. As new territories and islands were settled or conquered, the myths of the indigenous people were assimilated by the Greeks. Like those of other cultures, the deities of the ancient Greeks represented elements of nature, celestial bodies, and natural phenomena. Many of the myths were allegorical, depicting cycles of crops and origins of natural and man-made objects. More than in any other culture, however, the gods and goddesses personified human emotions and embodied attributes that the Greeks admired, disdained, and feared. Thus the Greek gods, while incredibly strong, proud, often honorable, intelligent, and beautiful, were also quarrelsome, headstrong, deceitful, jealous, and vain, and often embodied contradictory traits. Unlike their human counterparts, however, the gods had supernatural abilities, which they constantly wielded against each other and which allowed them to manipulate events on Earth from their home on Mt. Olympus.

The Storytellers

For centuries the Greek myths were passed down orally from parent to child; not until the blind poet Homer wrote the *Iliad* and the *Odyssey* in the mid–eighth century B.C., did a cohesive, interrelated narrative begin to emerge. Soon after, the poet Hesiod wrote *Theogony*, "the birth of the gods," which explains the origins of the gods and of the universe itself. Between 650 B.C. and 250 B.C., several different poets contributed to the thirty-three songs praising the gods called the *Homeric Hymns*. While some of these writers focused on retelling the myths for spiritual or philosophical purposes, many of these stories of the gods' exploits were written primarily for entertainment value, which distinguishes the Greeks from most other cultures whose motivations were more religious.

Indeed, from a religious standpoint, little is known about how the Greeks worshiped their gods. Temples were built to house the deities on their earthly visits, but the people weren't expected to pray there. Unlike those of most other cultures, the Greek gods were not demanding of the people of Earth. The gods did not like to be challenged or tricked, but they did not require worship by mortals to assure them a place in heaven. Small household shrines allowed the people to offer thanks to the gods who they believed walked among them.

Strength and Weakness in Zeus, the King of the Gods

According to Greek mythology, there were hundreds of gods and half gods. It was the twelve main Olympian gods, however, who presided over the world. These gods formed the Greek pantheon and were born soon after the universe was created by the Titans, the original race of gods whom Zeus overthrew in a ten-year battle for supremacy.

Armed with huge muscles and lightning bolts, Zeus was the strongest and most important figure in Greek myth. As the sky god and controller of the weather, he ruled over all the gods of Olympus and over humanity. It was also his job to act as judge

to settle disputes among the gods, which were numerous. Often Zeus himself was the cause of the quarrels, particularly with his wife, Hera, who often argued with him over his infidelities.

Zeus's attraction to women led to many intimate encounters with both goddesses and mortal women, out of which over a dozen immortals and dozens of mortals and half mortals were created. When Zeus came across a woman he wanted, he did not let anything stand in his way. He often changed his shape so that the unsuspecting woman would embrace him, not recognizing who he was. He turned himself into a cuckoo bird to win his wife, the goddess Hera. He became a swan to woo Leda, the queen of Sparta; a shower of gold to mate with Danae, the princess of Argos; a goatlike creature to win over Antiope, the daughter of a river god; and a bull to win over the Phoenician princess Europa. Most other women, either goddesses, nymphs, or Titans, did not need to be tricked into mating with him. It was prophesied that the offspring with his first wife, Metis, the Titan goddess of wisdom, would overthrow him one day. So before Metis gave birth, Zeus swallowed her. He soon developed a terrible headache and the god Hephaestus cut open Zeus's head. To their surprise, the goddess Athena sprang out, full grown and fully armed. At that time, however, Zeus was only beginning his adventures with women.

By mating with three different Titans, Zeus fathered the Fates, who determined the destinies of both humans and the gods; the Graces, who provided the world with beauty and charm; and the nine Muses, who

A Greek vase from the fifth century B.C. *features the sky god Zeus, the most important god in the Greek pantheon.*

inspired creativity in the arts and science. Though the Greeks' sense of moral conduct led them to disapprove of Zeus's infidelities, they were quick to lay claim to a family tree that possibly included Zeus as an ancestor. The Greeks also adored Hera, the ever-faithful wife, until she became obsessed with revenge and let her duties of protecting women in marriage and childbirth come second.

Maternity and Vengeance in Hera, the Mother Goddess

Hera was originally a mother goddess the Greeks incorporated into their pantheon from an older culture. She quickly became the most powerful goddess on Olympus, and the oldest temples in Greece were dedicated to her. She was the goddess of marriage and childbirth, and women prayed to her when

An illustration of the mother goddess Hera, the wife of Zeus, and the most powerful of the Greek goddesses.

princess Semele was pregnant, Hera disguised herself as a nurse and visited the young woman. Hera told Semele that if she really believed she had mated with Zeus, she should ask him to show her his true self. Semele did ask Zeus to reveal himself to her, and when he shone in all his bright glory, she burst into flames as a result. Zeus managed to save their unborn child, Dionysus, by sewing him up in his thigh, but Hera had won her revenge. Zeus was forced to turn another lover, Io, into a cow so that Hera would not recognize her. His trick did not work, however, and Hera sent a stinging insect after Io, who was then forced to run around the world in torment as a cow. Similarly, Hera changed the forest nymph Callisto into a bear (or Zeus changed her in the hopes of protecting her from Hera). Callisto, as the bear, was then shot by mistake by Artemis, one of Zeus's daughters by Leto.

Hera's need for revenge was seemingly inexhaustible. She forced another of Zeus's mistresses, Lamia, to eat her own offspring. For centuries, Lamia was thought by Greek children to be a vampire who ate bad little boys and girls. Hera even punished those who got in the way of her vengeance, like the nymph Echo, whose talking distracted her from catching Zeus with another mistress. Hera punished Echo by allowing her to speak only by repeating the words of others. This myth explains the origin of the word *echo*. Hera had four children, to whom she was indifferent, even as the god-

they wished to marry or start a family. As second in command next to her husband, Hera might have been quite content. Her downfall, however, was her jealousy.

Hera spent most of her time trying to punish Zeus's mistresses and their offspring. When she heard Zeus had impregnated the Titan goddess Leto, she ruled that Leto could not give birth either on land or sea, so Leto was forced to search the earth until she found a floating island where she gave birth to twins Apollo and Artemis. When the Theban dess of marriage and childbirth. Even Ares, who the Greeks believed was the incarnation of Hera's own anger, could not win her heart.

The Cruel and Immature Behavior of Ares, the God of War

Ares was arrogant, argumentative, brutal, and a bully. He joined gleefully into any battle he came across, not caring which side he fought on, or who won or lost. Whenever he got hurt—which was often since he was not very clever in battle—he cried like a baby and then went to his parents, Zeus and Hera, to heal him. Neither of them could stand their contemptible son, and they undertook the task of healing him grudgingly.

Once Ares was accused of killing the son of the sea god Poseidon, who he claimed was trying to hurt his own daughter Alcippe. The other gods wanted nothing more than for Ares to be found guilty so they could be rid of him, but Ares escaped punishment because no one witnessed the crime. The goddess Aphrodite was the only person who liked Ares, and they began a passionate affair. Caught in a compromising position by her husband, the god Hephaestos, they were forbidden to ever see each other again.

Ares was always jealous of his sister Athena, and complained loudly that his father (and everyone else) liked her better. He once attacked Athena in a childish rage, but she crushed him with a boulder and nearly killed him.

Proud and Giving Athena

Though the Greeks liked and respected Athena and worshiped her with the same

The Fall of the Mighty Titans

Before life existed there was only Chaos, a sea of nothingness. Out of this void came Gaia, the mother earth. She gave birth to Uranus, the god of the heavens. Together she and Uranus had twelve children called the Titans. Her last child was Cronos (or Kronos), who attacked his father and took over as ruler of the Titans. Cronos married his sister Rhea, who bore him six children, the first gods of Olympus. But after the first five had been born, Cronos swallowed them so that they would not rise up against him as had been prophesied. Rhea asked for help from her parents, Gaia and Uranus. They helped her hide her sixth child, Zeus, in a cave in Crete where Cronos would not look for him and where he was protected by a group of spirits called the Curetes who made so much noise that they drowned out the sounds of the child. She then presented Cronos with a large rock with blankets around it. Believing this was Zeus, he swallowed it. When Zeus grew to manhood, he tricked his father into throwing up his brothers and sisters along with the rock. He then led the Olympians into a violent ten-year battle until they vanquished Cronos and took control of the world.

loyalty accorded Hera, her odd birth set her apart. Aware that she was different from the other gods and goddesses, many of whom came into the world in a more traditional fashion, Athena was proud to have issued from her father Zeus's forehead. A warrior by nature, and a gifted strategist, Athena was primarily a protector of the people. She fought on the side of justice, introduced weaving and design, and watched over the Greek region of Attica.

A bust of the warrior goddess Athena, daughter of Zeus, and protector of the Greek people.

Usually very even-tempered, Athena's pride in her skills led to one young mortal woman's downfall. The maiden Arachne was known for her beautiful weaving, which she bragged was even better than the goddess Athena's. Athena disguised herself as an old woman and challenged Arachne to a contest. When Athena was forced to recognize that Arachne was the more skillful weaver, in a rare display of jealousy she turned the woman into a spider. More often, though, Athena helped mortals. She assisted Greek legendary heroes like Jason, Perseus, and Odysseus, and was particularly interested in the welfare of one specific city, which she won control over after a contest with Poseidon. Arguing over the city, they agreed that whoever gave the city the finest gift could claim it. Poseidon took his trident, hit the side of the Acropolis, and everyone watched as a spring of water appeared. Unfortunately, the salt water was not fit for drinking. Athena gave the city an olive tree, which in turn would provide food, oil, and wood for the people. She won the city, which she promptly named Athens. In response, Poseidon flooded the area surrounding the city itself.

Poseidon: Temperamental and Petty

Poseidon's reaction to losing the city of Athens to Athena was typical of his quarrelsome, greedy nature, which put him at odds with many of the other Olympians. Embittered by losing the right to rule the sky to his brother Zeus, he chose to live at the bottom

A mosaic of the temperamental sea god Poseidon brandishing his powerful three-pronged trident.

of the ocean rather than with the other gods in Olympus. His rule was over the vast seas, although he was also the god of earthquakes and horses. Poseidon was worshiped by sailors, who believed he protected their boats from turbulent waters and dangerous marauders. A very temperamental character, however, Poseidon would use his powerful three-pronged trident to cause earthquakes and shipwrecks as easily as he would provide calm seas and new islands for lost ships to reach the shore.

He and his brother Zeus had a lot in common when it came to women. Just like Zeus, Poseidon fathered many children whether or not the woman was a willing participant. He even mated with the evil snake-haired Medusa, which resulted in the winged horse Pegasus. But his greatest challenge was Demeter, the goddess of crops and fertility. To avoid Poseidon's advances, Demeter changed herself into a female horse. Poseidon responded by turning himself into a stallion and overpowering her. He later became infatuated with a sea nymph named Amphitrite and was determined to marry her. She, however, was not interested in being his wife and ran away. Poseidon

Hesiod's *Theogony*

In the eighth century B.C. the Greek poet, theologian, and philosopher Hesiod wrote an epic poem, *Theogony* (translated here by Richmond Lattimore), a major source of information about the Greek gods and goddesses. It begins:

Let us begin our singing, from the Helikonian Muses who possess the great and holy mountain of Helikon and dance there on soft feet by the dark blue water of the spring, and by the altar of the powerful son of Kronos; who wash their tender bodies in the waters of Permessos; from there they rise, and put a veiling of deep mist upon them, and walk in the night, singing in sweet voices, and celebrating Zeus, the holder of the aegis, and Hera, his lady of Argos, who treads on golden sandals, and singing also Athene the gray-eyed daughter of Zeus of the aegis, Phoibos Apollo, and Artemis of the showering arrow, Poseidon who encircles the earth in his arms and shakes it, stately Themis, and Aphrodite of the fluttering eyelids, Hebe of the golden wreath, beautiful Dione, Leto and Iapetos and devious-devising Kronos, Eos, the dawn, great Helios, and shining Selene, Gaia, the earth and great Okeanos, and dark Night, and all the holy rest of the everlasting immortals. And it was they who once taught Hesiod his splendid singing, as he was shepherding his lambs on holy Helikon, and these were the first words of all the goddesses spoke to me, the Muses of Olympia, daughters of Zeus of the aegis: You shepherds of the wilderness, poor fools, nothing but bellies, we know how to say many false things that seem like true sayings, but we know also how to speak the truth when we wish to.

sent a dolphin to find her and bring her back. Having no other choice, and being somewhat impressed by his perseverance, the nymph married Poseidon and bore him three children.

Poseidon and Zeus had one other brother, Hades, the god of the dead and of riches. Hades chose not to leave the underworld often, even to visit the other gods on Olympus. Hades was not as aggressive a womanizer as his brothers. He set his sights on one woman, the goddess Persephone (also known as Kore), but he had to deal with her mother, Demeter, first.

Devotion and Growth: Demeter

Demeter was the goddess of agriculture, responsible for growing plants, trees, grains, and fruits. Her devotion to her daughter Persephone (whose father was Zeus) led to the creation of winter. According to myth, Zeus's brother Hades fell in love with Persephone and asked Demeter for her daughter's hand in marriage. Demeter refused to grant it, believing Persephone was too young to be married, and that Hades was not a suitable mate. Hades did not like this response, and one day while Persephone was out picking flowers, Hades burst through the ground in his chariot, kidnapped her, and brought her to the underworld. Like the earth, the underworld had rivers (some made of fire) and land, trees, and caves. The longest river, the Styx, circled the underworld nine times. When mortals died they were ferried along the Styx to be judged. If they were deemed blameless, they traveled to the beautiful Elysian Fields. If not, they were

A stone relief from the fifth century B.C. depicts Demeter, the goddess of agriculture, and her daughter by Zeus, Persephone (right).

sent to either Erebos or Tartaros to be punished. As Hades' consort, Persephone was supposed to rule the underworld with him. Grief-stricken Demeter searched everywhere for her beloved daughter. In her sorrow she let all the plants on the earth wither. Nothing grew, no animals multiplied, and life on Earth was threatened.

Zeus finally stepped in and told Hades he had to return the girl to her mother, but only if she had not eaten anything while down in the underworld. Since he wanted her to stay, Hades gave Persephone a pomegranate seed to eat. When Demeter learned of Hades' trickery, she was so angry and distraught that Zeus quickly came up with a compromise. Persephone had to remain with Hades for one-third of the year as the goddess of the underworld, but could join her mother on Earth for the rest. When Persephone was reunited with Demeter, the plants grew again and the crops were revitalized. For the three months of the year when Persephone returned to Hades, the season of winter, Demeter's sorrow made the land barren. The Greeks knew that when Persephone returned to her mother, the earth would once again be green.

The Joy, Revelry, and Violence of Dionysus

Another deity who was separated from his mother was Dionysus. Although the last god to be admitted into the Olympic pantheon, he was originally worshiped in Crete as early as the fifteenth century B.C. The son of Zeus, he emerged from his father's thigh after the death of his mother, the mortal woman Semele. To protect the child from his jealous wife, Zeus turned him into a goat for a while and left him to the nymphs to raise. Dionysus soon learned he had the power to make wine and became known as the god of the vine, sexuality, and joyous behavior. He traveled through many countries, followed by a cult of odd characters including centaurs, satyrs, nymphs, and maenads, women who worked themselves into an ecstatic frenzy. Although gentle and loving to his followers, anyone who refused Dionysus's company or turned away his companions was severely punished. Sometimes drunken followers ran through the forest with wild abandon, destroying every living creature in their way.

When Dionysus eventually assumed his place on Olympus, he was allowed to bring back his mother from the underworld. The pantheon of the gods of Olympus was now complete. But while the real Mount Olympus will forever loom over the Greek horizon, the gods were doomed to fade into memory.

Fall from Grace

In most cultures, only foreign invasion leads people to stop believing in their own gods. But in ancient Greece, the gods fell out of favor long before the spread of Christianity. By the time of Plato, around 400 B.C., the Greeks were starting to recognize that the gods and their stories were steeped in symbolism and allegory, and as scientific discovery progressed, they began to understand the true basis of natural phenomena. Although the deities gradually became regarded as cultural icons, they

Apollo and the Oracle at Delphi

As the god of light, poetry, medicine, music, and prophecy, Apollo was very important to the Greeks. In the Homeric Hymns, written between 650 and 250 B.C. and translated here by Apostolos N. Athanassakis, Apollo's mother, Leto, makes a promise to the island where she gives birth. Apollo himself then pledges to keep his mother's promise to build his famous Oracle at Delphi, where men and women came to find the answers to their futures:

Leto: Earth be my witness and the wide heaven above
and the cascading water of the Styx, which is the greatest
and most awful oath among the blessed gods,
that here there shall always be a fragrant altar and temple
for Phoibos [Aploos] and that he shall honor you above all others.

Apollo: Here I intend to build a beautiful temple
to be an oracle for men who shall always
bring to this place unblemished hecatombs;
and as many as dwell on fertile Peloponnesos
and on Europe and throughout the sea-girt
islands will consult it. It is my wish to give them
unerring advice, making prophecies inside the
opulent temple.

When a visitor asked the priestess of the temple a question, she would enter a trance state and respond with cryptic answers, which the visitor was then left to interpret. Many important events in the history of Greek mythology took place because of the oracle's prophecies, including actions by Heracles, Oedipus, King Croesus, and Aeneas. Greek scholars would meet there for intellectual discussions, and beautiful artifacts—gifts from those hoping for a positive response from the oracle—were on display. Christian rulers put an end to the oracle in 400 A.D.

A man consults a priestess at the Oracle at Delphi.

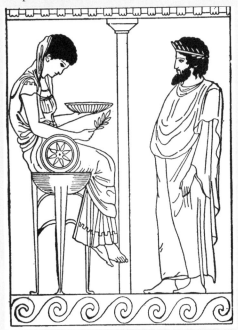

remained deeply ingrained in Greek civilization. The exploits of the larger-than-life Greek gods and goddesses continue to affect life in the twenty-first century through art, literature, philosophy, and psychology. Their tales of joy and pain, full of emotion and drama, of conflict and celebration, revenge and aid, are at once universal and distinctive to Greece, the most advanced society in the ancient world.

Roman Deities: Reflecting the Fortunes of the Empire

For twelve hundred years the Roman Empire controlled much of Europe and the Mediterranean world. Skilled administrators more than innovators, however, the Romans adopted much of their religion and mythology from other cultures, including the Greeks, Egyptians, Persians, Syrians, Sabines, and Etruscans. From these foreign gods, the Romans organized their own pantheon to suit their needs. They created and manipulated their collection of deities and their corresponding myths to justify, explain, and preserve the existence of the Roman Empire. The history of their gods and goddesses is virtually inseparable from the rise and fall of the empire itself.

The city that was to be the seat of the vast Roman Empire actually began with a few Latin shepherds settling around the Tiber River in Italy in the eighth century B.C. Eventually the settlement of Rome grew, greatly influenced by the Etruscan culture to the north and by the Greeks who had already built communities in southern Italy and Sicily. In these early centuries, the Romans practiced no organized religion. Rather, they believed that a powerful divine spirit resided in each natural and man-made object.

The Old Spirit Gods

In the early Empire, the Romans thought of their deities as formless ideas and concepts, rather than as gods having human form. Each element of nature had a spirit that was to be respected. They referred to this spirit as *numin*, and collectively these spirits (or gods) were known as *numina*. It was important to maintain a good, peaceful relationship with the *numina*, so these formless deities were prayed to often and praised for their continued protection. The *numina* existed to carry out a particular function, and were not assigned stories, personalities, or family genealogies as were the gods of other cultures. Their role was purely utilitarian, and

they could be discarded if their service was deemed no longer necessary.

Within Roman households, a number of household gods had to be placated. The male head of each family acted as the mediator between the other family members and the household gods. Three types of spirits were worshiped at household shrines, called larariums: The lares protected the family's property and land, the penates protected the food

Ancient Romans worshiped household gods with offerings of food and drink at shrines called lorariums, like the one pictured here.

supply in the cupboards, and the genii (or genius) were the inner spirits of the people and objects in the house. All of these spirits had to be attended to with offerings of food and drink. As Rome advanced and the people left their agricultural roots behind, their needs changed and new gods were identified to support those changes. The Romans suddenly needed gods for objects they had not seen before, and for endeavors they had not attempted before. They were quick to adopt foreign gods who might be able to help them in their growth.

Janus Links the *Numina* and the New Pantheon

By the time the Romans were organized and powerful enough to carry on campaigns of conquest, the gods and goddesses of the Greek culture were well established in all neighboring lands. The Romans decided to weave their own history into the already existing mythology of the Greeks and Etruscans. They gradually gave human forms to the *numina* and began to turn many of the Greek deities into Roman gods and goddesses. By the second century B.C., the Greek pantheon had been fully Romanized. This meant not only that Greek names had been changed to Roman ones, but also that some of the more violent and immoral attributes of the Greek gods had been eliminated.

It was the rare god who maintained his original utilitarian purpose once the Romans

Janus, the god of doorways and beginnings, is always pictured with two faces—one looking forward to the future and one peering backward to the past.

adopted the Greek pantheon. One such god was Janus, the god of doorways and beginnings. Janus was always pictured with two heads, one looking forward to the future, one backward to the past, and holding a key in his right hand. His good graces were invoked at the start of a new project, a birth, a marriage, planting season, or simply when walking through an entrance or gate. In times of war, the doors of his temple within the Roman Forum were always kept open so Janus would be able to lead the gods to assist in battle. Closed doors indicated a rare peace prevailed over the land. Janus was also thought of as the first creator god and the first ruler of Italy. The Janiculum, one of the seven hills of Rome, and the month of January were both named in his honor.

During the reign of Augustus (27 B.C.–14 A.D.), Rome enjoyed a golden age politically and culturally. Augustus wanted the people to feel pride in the Empire, and encouraged monumental construction and literature that lauded the glory of Rome. He placed the gods Mars and Apollo in highest esteem, since they most fully embodied his vision. It was during this period that the first real Roman myth, the epic poem *Aeneid*, was written by the poet Virgil. Encouraged by Augustus, Virgil based his twelve-book epic on the Greek writer Homer's *Odyssey* and *Iliad*, and tied together the threads of ancient history in such a way as to make the Roman Empire seem preordained and blessed by the gods. Through Virgil's patriotic, mythic hero Aeneas—who was already a character in the original Greek myth of the events following the Trojan War—he mixed politics, mythology, and history to create a new legend: the tale of the birth and glory of Rome. The most important Roman gods were the ones directly associated with Aeneas's story.

Following Virgil, other writers such as the poet Horace and the historian Livy also helped establish Rome's dominance. Their work, favored highly by Augustus, allowed the Romans to justify the right of the Empire to assert its power over everyone else. Soon after, the emperors began claiming to be descended from the gods, especially from the goddess Venus, and each emperor was deified (regarded as a god) after his death and took his place among the protectors of Rome.

While they were alive, many emperors expected to be treated as if they were gods already.

Venus Protects Aeneas and Torments Psyche

The goddess Venus was so admired throughout Rome's history that Julius Caesar and Augustus claimed to be descended from her, and many great leaders dedicated temples in her name, including the Roman general Pompey and the emperor Hadrian. Originally an agricultural goddess, she later became associated with the Greek goddess Aphrodite and took on the attributes of the goddess of love. One day Venus had an affair with a mortal man named Anchises and gave birth to Aeneas, the man whose descendants would be the founders of Rome. Aeneas was the definitive Roman hero— brave, pious, and dedicated to his goal, founding a new empire. He needed Venus, however, to help him get out of some very dangerous situations when all hope for his survival would surely have been lost. She intervened on his behalf when the other gods were not willing to help him, and retrieved his spear in battle when he otherwise would have been cut down by the great warrior Turnis at the very end of the *Aeneid*. For these acts she was elevated to her high status, and was considered the mother of the Roman people.

Because of the status of Venus, her son Cupid was bound to play an important role in Roman mythology. As told by the poet Ovid in his collection of myths, the *Metamorphoses*, Cupid, the young god of love,

Vesta and the Vestal Virgins

Considered the guardian of the city of Rome, the goddess Vesta was honored by a round temple built in the Forum in the third century B.C. As goddess of the hearth, her temple housed an ever-burning flame (brought by Aeneas from Troy) that was carefully tended by four (later six) women called Vestal Virgins. These women were selected from Rome's upper-class families before they were ten years old. They guarded the perpetual flame, performed related rituals, and kept their virginity at all costs. The Vestals also oversaw the festival of Vestalia every June 9. If the sacred flame ever went out, they were whipped, often to death. If at any time during their thirty-year term they gave up their virginity, they were first whipped and then buried alive in a small underground tomb. If they did their jobs well, their life could be quite pleasant. In fact, they were allowed to stay on after their thirty-year tenure was over, and most did.

A third-century statue of the goddess Vesta, considered the guardian of the city of Rome.

helped Venus in her matchmaking endeavors by shooting love arrows at his mother's chosen target. Sometimes, however, Venus's schemes did not turn out as planned. For instance, Venus was once jealous of a beautiful mortal girl named Psyche and sent Cupid to make the girl fall in love with the worst man on Earth. Cupid fell in love with Psyche instead, infuriating his mother. During their affair, Cupid had instructed Psyche not to look at him in the light, but Psyche could not resist. Cupid had no choice but to leave her,

A painting shows Cupid, the god of love, visiting Psyche. According to myth, Venus sent Cupid to make Psyche fall in love with another man but Cupid fell in love with her instead.

and she was heartbroken. She braved the wrath of Venus by asking the goddess for help in finding the missing Cupid. Venus assigned Psyche nearly impossible tasks, which the girl managed to perform on the verge of giving up. In the end love prevailed, Cupid came to her aid, and Psyche was made immortal. Venus eventually accepted Psyche as her daughter-in-law and was glad that her son Cupid was happy.

Mars and the Founders of Rome

Like Venus, the god Mars was originally based on an ancient agricultural god. He became known as the god of war once he was paired with the Greek god Ares. Mars was considered the father of the Roman people because of the part he played in the founding of the city of Rome. It all started with a mortal princess named Rhea Silvia. She had been forced by her uncle to become a vestal virgin, a woman who serves the goddess Vesta and does not mate with men. Her uncle did not want any children of hers to take the throne away from him. Although she had vowed not to, she mated with Mars and became pregnant with twin boys. When the twins, Romulus and Remus, were born, they were thrown into the Tiber River to drown. Luckily, they were rescued by a shepherd and fed milk by a she-wolf. The twins knew they wanted to establish a new city on the spot where they had been rescued, but were very competitive with each other. Romulus decided to kill Remus and named the new city Rome, after himself. According to Virgil's *Aeneid*, this happened in the year 753 B.C. To populate the city, Romulus kidnapped women from the neighboring Sabine tribes who had come to Rome for a celebration. This act provoked a war until the father of the gods, Jupiter, intervened on Rome's behalf and peace was restored.

As the father of Rome's founder, Mars enjoyed a special place as the second most important god in the Roman pantheon

A sculpture of Romulus and Remus drinking milk from a she-wolf after being rescued depicts the story of the founding of Rome.

(Jupiter was first), a much higher spot than his Greek counterpart. He played a more protective role than Ares, and soldiers made offerings to him both before and after battles. The Romans admired Mars's traits of courage, strength, and justice, especially during the reign of Augustus, who believed that Mars symbolized everything the Romans should strive to become. He was so important to the Romans that the month of March, originally the first month of the calendar, was named after him.

Jupiter, Juno, and Minerva: A Trio Worthy of the Romans

Jupiter (or Jove), the king of the gods, retained all the grandeur of his Greek counterpart Zeus while refraining from much of his immoral, womanizing behavior. Jupiter was also the god of light, of the sky, of justice,

The Beginnings of Virgil's *Aeneid*

The *Aeneid*, written in approximately 19 B.C. by the Roman poet Virgil, combined the real history of the ancient world and existing Greek myths to create something totally new—the divine history of the Roman Empire. The *Aeneid*, translated here by John Dryden, is twelve books long, and begins with the hero Aeneas's exile from Troy:

Arms, and the man I sing, who, forc'd by fate,
And haughty Juno's unrelenting hate,
Expell'd and exil'd, left the Trojan shore.
Long labors, both by sea and land, he bore,
And in the doubtful war, before he won
The Latian realm, and built the destin'd town;
His banish'd gods restor'd to rites divine,
And settled sure succession in his line,
From whence the race of Alban fathers come,
And the long glories of majestic Rome.
O Muse! the causes and the crimes relate;
What goddess was provok'd, and whence her hate;
For what offense the Queen of Heav'n began
To persecute so brave, so just a man;
Involv'd his anxious life in endless cares,
Expos'd to wants, and hurried into wars!
Can heav'nly minds such high resentment show,
Or exercise their spite in human woe?

and victory in battle. Like Mars, whom some consider Jupiter's son though he was not directly involved in Mars's conception, his status was elevated as a result of his role in helping Romulus protect Rome against the Sabines during Rome's inception. Although he played a small role in Roman myths, his power and position was never questioned. Jupiter's main temple was not only a place for the people to worship, but also a meeting place where politicians declared wars and arranged truces.

Outside Rome, his temples occupied the most sought-after spots in the Roman Empire, although he shared many of them with his wife Juno and his daughter Minerva, who was originally an Etruscan craft goddess. Like the Greek Athena, Minerva had sprung forth fully formed and armed from her father's forehead. Although, like her father, she did not figure in many myths, she did preside over the Romans as the goddess of crafts, arts, medicine, wisdom, and—in keeping with her association with Athena—war. Together Jupiter, Juno, and Minerva were known as the Capitoline Triad, and the popular trio were often worshiped collectively by sacrificing animals like oxen and horses.

As queen of the gods, Juno was considered a kinder woman than her Greek counterpart, Hera, although she did possess some of the same jealousy. As Mars symbolized favorable male qualities, Juno represented the qualities Roman women sought. She was stately and beautiful, and protected women in marriage and childbirth. When Juno learned that the goddess Minerva had been born directly from Jupiter's head, she became jealous and

decided to conceive a child of her own. The minor goddess Flora rubbed herbs on Juno's stomach and she became pregnant with Mars.

Although much loved by the Romans, Juno was not always benevolent. She made Aeneas's journey more difficult by throwing obstacles in his path, and her jealousy led to the half-mortal Hercules' famous Twelve Labors. Also, when she learned that the goddess Leto was pregnant by her husband, Jupiter, she decreed that Leto would not give birth anywhere on land. Leto finally found a small island and gave birth to the twins Diana and Apollo. Diana, the Romanized version of the Greek goddess Artemis, became the goddess of the hunt and of the woods. Apollo reflected the Greek god of the same name yet achieved prominence as the ideal Roman god.

Apollo and Cybele: A Good Role Model and a Bad One

Like Mars, the god Apollo symbolized the greatness the Roman Empire hoped to achieve. As a gesture of fellowship, the Romans did not change the name of the Greek Apollo, making him unique in the new pantheon. They focused on Apollo's role as the sun god, who would herald in a new age of prosperity and peace as he drove the sun across the heavens. The son of Jupiter and Leto (one of the Greek Titans), he was initially worshiped as the god of healing, later as the god of music, the arts, prophecy, and archery. Although considered extremely handsome, Apollo was unlucky in

An illustration of Diana, goddess of the hunt and of the woods, riding in a chariot.

love. In one of his failed love affairs he lost forever the nymph Daphne when her father protected her by changing her into a laurel tree. From then on, long-haired Apollo wore a wreath of laurel leaves around his head in the memory of his lost love. For a long time boys in Rome let their hair grow long in imitation of Apollo.

In keeping with the tradition of adopting foreign gods as long as they could be useful in the Romans' current situation, an ancient neolithic goddess from what is today Turkey made her Roman debut in 204 B.C., and promptly became too much for the Roman government to handle. Riding in her lion-drawn chariot accompanied by clashing cymbals and dancers, Cybele, later referred to as Magna Mater, became a powerful fertility and mother goddess. It was written in the Sibylline Books (a collection of prophetic books that reportedly foretold the history of Rome) that Cybele should be brought to Rome to save the city from Hannibal's invading forces in the Second Punic War. Her consort Attis was sometimes referred to as a god of vegetation, and other times as a mortal man born on December 25, a date later recognized in the Christian religion as the birth of Christ. The cult of Cybele was worshiped with

The Roman Adaptations of the Greek Olympians

When the Romans adopted the Greek gods, they renamed them (except for Apollo) and gave them more distinctly Roman characteristics. Many of them were not as popular or important as they were to the Greeks, but others (like Mars/Ares and Vesta/Hestia) were even more so.

Jupiter/Zeus: king of the gods, sky god
Juno/Hera: queen of the gods, mother goddess
Mars/Ares: god of war
Vesta/Hestia: goddess of the hearth
Cupid/Eros: god of love
Minerva/Athena: goddess of wisdom, crafts, and war
Diana/Artemis: goddess of the hunt, goddess of the moon
Vulcan/Hephaestus: god of fire and the forge
Mercury/Hermes: god of commerce, messenger god
Neptune/Poseidon: god of the sea
Ceres/Demeter: goddess of the crops
Proserpina/Persephone: goddess of the underworld
Bacchus/Dionysus: god of wine and fertility

The Roman goddess Juno, known as Hera in the Greek pantheon.

such wild celebrations that the Roman government was forced to forbid them for two centuries. Emperor Claudius then officially made a more relaxed form of Cybele worship an accepted part of the Roman religion. With the onset of Christianity, however, there was no room for the original Roman gods, to say nothing of the imported ones.

Rome Embraces Its Final God

The Romans did not easily give up their gods and the introduction of Christianity into Rome was anything but smooth. At first only a small number of Romans converted to Christianity, although the concept of a single supreme god did make sense to those who believed the Roman gods were more symbolic than anything else. For the first few centuries A.D., the Christians were persecuted on and off for refusing to worship the ancient gods or accepting the deity of dead emperors. Eventually the tide turned, and it became the Christians who persecuted those who still worshiped pagan (pre-Christian) gods.

A depiction of the popular fertility and mother goddess Cybele, who was worshiped for years with wild celebrations.

Whenever one religion supplants another, some of the former's traditions are adopted to smooth the transition. The early Christian church based its major holidays on formerly existing ones. Some Christian saints were likewise based on ancient deities and in Rome the initial images of Jesus bore a remarkable resemblance to statues of Apollo, while Mary resembled images of the goddess Isis, whose cult had been brought from Egypt.

Today the Roman Catholic Church is centered in Rome's Vatican City, the headquarters of the Catholic religion and the home of the pope, the religious leader who is believed to be God's representative on Earth. The ancient spirit gods, the gods of the pantheon adapted from the Greeks, and the imported deities like Cybele and Isis are respected as a part of Rome's history, but have all long been laid to rest.

Viking Deities: The Ideals of a Warrior Culture

In the old Teutonic language of northern Europe, the word *Viking* meant "fighting men" or "raiders," and the term *Norsemen* meant "men from the north." These two interchangeable terms refer to the society that was initially a community of Germanic tribes that settled in Scandinavia (Norway, Denmark, and Sweden) around the middle of the eighth century A.D. Once established, these expert sailors and brave explorers quickly raided England, Ireland, and Scotland in search of riches, more land, and a better life. The Vikings of the next century went on to raid Italy, Spain, North Africa, Russia, and Germany. During that time as many as ten thousand Vikings left Norway and created a settlement in Iceland. Soon after, in 980 A.D., Erik the Red discovered Greenland and many kinsmen followed him there. In the lands they settled, the Vikings endured harsh, hazardous winters, a scarcity of food, and even perpetual darkness

during much of the year. They became a hardy, tough, and resigned people well aware that the elements of nature could quickly and suddenly end their lives. This cultural environment led to the creation of deities who embodied not only the forces of nature, but the violence and uncertainty of the Vikings' everyday life.

A proud, fierce, and passionate group, the Vikings created their deities in their own image, only with their strengths magnified. Although they bore vague similarities to the Celtic and Greek gods, and were sometimes based on myths already known in Scandinavia, the Norse deities were primarily reflections of the ideals this fierce culture valued and the hardships it feared. These exaggerated humanlike warriors succeeded in their tasks by force, treachery, and magic. Each central deity characterized some element of the struggle for success, differing greatly in approach. The two branches of deities—the

Aesir (sky gods) and the Vanir (earth gods)—were, like the Vikings themselves, always in battle, either with foreign invaders, monsters, giants, or each other. And unlike almost every other known mythology, these deities were not immortal. If they were, the Vikings would not have been able to feel the gods were truly brave in the face of death, which was something they demanded not only of their gods, but of themselves. The violence of their gods helped the Vikings justify the violence of their own society.

Explorer Erik the Red kills an Icelandic chief. Erik the Red discovered Greenland and founded a Viking settlement there.

Odin Rules with Wisdom and Savagery

Among the Viking Aesir gods, the ruler was Odin (also known as Woden), who assumed his role at his birth at the beginning of creation. Out of the great void known as Ginnungagap, there arose regions of ice in the north and fire in the south. These regions joined to form Ymir, the frost giant and the first living creature. From Ymir came another giant named Buri. Buri's son Bor had three sons who were not giants, but gods. These three sons, Odin, Vili, and Ve, started the first conflict by conspiring together to kill Ymir. Almost all of the other giants died in the river created by Ymir's blood. Those who lived became the gods' enemies. The three brothers used Ymir's body to form the earth and the heavens. After creating Asgard, their new home, they fashioned the first man and woman out of fallen tree trunks. The man was named Ask ("ash") and the woman Embla ("elm"). The new couple was then sent to middle-earth, Midgard, to populate the human race.

Of the original three gods, Odin became the most powerful. Often called All-Father, this god of death, war, and wisdom resided in Valhalla, the great hall where slain warriors waited for the day Odin would lead them in

Odin, the powerful god of death, war, and wisdom, and the ruler of the Viking gods, is pictured sitting on his throne.

How the Universe Was Constructed

Although made in their image, the gods did not live among humans. The Viking concept of how the universe was constructed was very detailed. Every element of life had a home somewhere in the Vikings' three-leveled universal structure.

Set up very much like three round plates suspended vertically in the air, these three levels contained nine distinct worlds held together by the roots of a tree called Yggdrasil. The upper level was called Asgard, and housed the Aesir gods. This level also contained Valhalla, the huge hall where dead warriors fought each day and feasted each night as they waited for Ragnarok, the final battle. The world of men was located in the center of the middle layer, called Midgard, and was connected to Asgard by a flaming rainbow bridge called Bifrost. In the huge ocean that surrounded Midgard lived the World Serpent Jormungand, who circled completely around Midgard and bit his own tail. Jotunheim and the fortress Utgard, the world where the giants lived, was either located on the eastern coast of Midgard or across the sea. The giants were also believed to live in the roots of the Yggdrasil tree, where they were responsible for earthquakes and volcanoes.

the final battle between the giants and the gods called Ragnarok (which translates as "twilight of the gods"). Able to see the future, Odin knew he would be killed in that battle by the wolf Fenrir, but he prepared vigorously nonetheless. Each day the dead warriors (called Einheriar) practiced fighting until they were "killed" again. Then at the evening meal the dead warriors would be served a feast which would bring them back to "life." Some Viking warriors, still very much alive, were so inspired by Odin's bravery in war that they rushed naked and fearless into battles. These men, nicknamed "berserkers," claimed to feel no pain when struck by their enemy.

Odin was not only worshiped for his fighting skills and lust for battles but also looked to for his wisdom and magical abilities. From his throne he could see all of the world, and each day he sent his two ravens, Munnin ("memory") and Huginn ("thought") to gather information about the people's needs. He was also fortunate to own three items that helped him win battles: a magic spear called Gungnir, which never missed its target; an eight-footed horse named Sleipnir; and a magic ring called Draupnir, which provided everlasting riches by reproducing itself eight times every nine days.

In his quest for wisdom, Odin sacrificed one of his eyes to the giant Mimir in exchange for a sip from the fountain of knowledge. For more wisdom, he pierced the side of his body with his spear and hung

The Strength and Fearlessness of Thor

Thor, god of weather, crops, and justice, wields his powerful hammer.

The strongest of the gods, and second in greatness only to his father, Odin, red-bearded Thor was the popular god of the weather, crops, and justice. His main job was to protect mankind from the giants, which he accomplished with help from a magic belt that made him twice as strong as he already was. His main source of his fighting prowess, however, was his magical boomerang-like hammer (called Mjollnir), which, when thrown at his enemy, always returned to Thor's iron-gloved hand.

Thor's wife, the corn goddess Sif, was indirectly responsible for her husband's receiving his hammer in the first place. One night the tricky and unreliable god Loki cut off Sif's long golden hair as a practical joke. Thor was so angry he demanded Loki replace the hair. Loki found two brothers who made Sif a wig of spun gold that attached itself to her head as soon as she put it on. Two dwarf brothers claimed they could make something just as impressive, and they did—the magic hammer that Loki delivered as a gift to Thor. With his hammer, Thor was able to defeat giants and to keep the evil serpent Jormungand, who surrounded the world of man, at bay. When the Vikings heard thunder, they were assured

himself from the Yggdrasil tree (the tree of life) for nine agonizing days. For his bravery and endurance he was granted knowledge of the runes, a symbolic magical language, which now gave him more ways to help mankind. For all Odin's sacrifices, the Vikings believed they needed to offer human sacrifices in his name. Because of Odin's rather terrifying nature, he received respect from the Vikings, but not adoration. That level of devotion was reserved for the mighty Thor, the son of Odin and Gaia.

that Thor was doing his job. It was even fashionable for the Vikings to wear hammer-shaped charms around their necks to invoke Thor's strength.

To the Vikings, however, there was no such thing as total invincibility. Thor needed Loki's help to regain ownership of his magic hammer, which had fallen into the hands of the giant Thrym. Thrym told Thor he would return the hammer on one condition: Thor must give him the Vanir goddess Freya to be his wife. Freya did not like this agreement, but Loki came up with an plan: He suggested that Thor go to Thrym disguised as Freya, and they would trick Thrym into returning the hammer. Thor agreed, and he and Loki went to Thrym's hall with Thor dressed as the goddess. At dinner, Thrym expressed surprise at how much food Freya (really Thor) ate. Loki explained that Freya was so excited to marry him she had not eaten for nine days. He explained Thor's red complexion by saying Freya had not slept and was feverish with anticipation. Thrym, fooled by these deceptions, laid the hammer on Thor's lap. Thor instantly picked it up and slew all the giants in the hall.

The Vikings prophesied that at Ragnarok, Thor's strength would eventually run out. Although he would kill Jormungand by striking the serpent's head with his hammer, the poisonous venom that poured out of the serpent's mouth would drown him.

All Praise Balder

Snorri Sturluson, the thirteenth-century Icelandic poet and chieftan, began the *Prose Edda* in 1220 A.D., over a century after the Viking period had ended. The stories and legends about the Viking gods found in the *Prose Edda* are the best source of Viking lore in existence. This excerpt, translated by Arthur Gilchrist Brodeur, shows how much the god Balder was loved:

Then said Gangleri: I would ask tidings of more Aesir. Harr replied: The second son of Odin is Baldr, and good things are to be said of him. He is best, and all praise him; he is so fair of feature, and so bright, that light shines from him. A certain herb is so white that it is likened to Baldr's brow; of all grasses it is whitest, and by it thou mayest judge his fairness, both in hair and in body. He is the wisest of the Aesir, and the fairest-spoken and most gracious; and that quality attends him, that none may gain-say his judgments. He dwells in the place called Breidablik, which is in heaven; in that place may nothing unclean be, even as it is said here:

Breidablik t'is called, where Baldr has
A hall made for himself:
In that land where I know lie
Fewest baneful runes.

Loki's Trickery

Loki, the fire god, did not start out as villainous. In the beginning, he was welcomed into Asgard, the home of the gods, even though his parents were giants. The Vikings respected him because he was able to defeat his enemies by using his wits and his ability to physically transform himself into other creatures. Out of boredom, he began to play tricks and pranks on the other gods, and a few times he even helped them by tricking their enemies. Loki's tricky nature was best highlighted in his participation in a scheme involving apples the gods needed to remain youthful. To get himself out of a tight spot with a giant named Thiassi, he agreed to steal the magic apples from the goddess Idun, whose job it was to gather and dispense them. Loki tricked the young woman into following him into the woods, where Thiassi grabbed her. Without their daily apples, however, the gods were beginning to die. Loki acted as confused as all the other gods about what had happened to Idun and her apples. He then turned himself into a falcon and stole Idun back from the giant. When he returned to Asgard, the other gods believed he was a hero.

Loki eventually developed an evil aspect, however, and three of his children—the serpent Jormungand, the wolf Fenrir, and the goddess Hel, who was half alive and half dead—reflected his evil ways. It was Odin's job to keep these three evil creatures away from the world of men. He threw the serpent into the ocean, where it wrapped itself around the earth, assigned Hel to watch over the netherworld called Nelheim, and bound Fenrir to a rock.

At the height of his evil, Loki managed to make a lifelong enemy of Odin's wife Frigga for the part he played in her son Balder's death. Odin vowed he would make Loki pay for his behavior. When Odin realized Loki had turned himself into a salmon, he led his son Thor to the brook where the salmon was hiding. Thor caught Loki with a net and bound him to the rocks. A serpent was then suspended above him which dripped poisonous venom on his face. Loki's wife Sigyn tried to collect the venom in a cup so it would not land on her husband, but spilled it on him by mistake. Loki would be released from the rock to fight at Ragnarok, where he would perish along with the others.

Frigga's Supervision and Balder's Perfection

Odin's wife, Frigga (or Frigg), was a marriage and fertility goddess. Although, like her husband, she could foresee the future, she kept silent and would not share her visions. Known also as the goddess of the sky, she lived in her own palace, called Fensalir, where she created the clouds through her weaving. Frigga's greatest need was to protect her son Balder, who was beloved by the Vikings. That she failed in this task brought her endless misery and set the world on its path toward Ragnarok.

Although Balder had little power as a god, he was adored by men and gods alike. Known as the god of joy, beauty, innocence, and light, Balder was considered a kind, nonaggressive deity. While still a young man, Balder had nightmares of his own death. Frightened, he told his mother Frigga about it. She immediately sprang into action and

An illustration depicts Loki bound to a rock, while his wife Sigyn tries to collect the venom of the snake that hangs above him.

made every living thing in the world promise not to harm him. The one item she overlooked was a small bush of mistletoe. The other gods made a game of throwing things at their beloved Balder, just to watch them harmlessly bounce off of him. But Loki, in his evil mode, was jealous of Balder. Using his shape-shifting ability, Loki turned himself into an old woman and tricked Frigga into telling him why Balder suddenly could not be harmed. She revealed that the only thing she had not asked not to harm him was the mistletoe, because it was so small and weak. Armed with that knowledge, Loki tricked Balder's blind twin brother, Hodr, into hurling a branch of the mistletoe at his brother as part of the gods' game. The branch punctured Balder and killed him.

Tricked by the jealous Loki, Hodr shoots a branch of mistletoe at his brother Balder, killing him.

While the world mourned the loss, Frigga took action. She sent her son Hermod into the netherworld, ruled over by Loki's daughter, the goddess Hel, to beg for Balder's release. Hel said the only way she would restore Balder's life was if every creature in all the world would weep for him. Every creature did weep, except for Loki. Unable to be brought back to life without Loki's tears, his body, along with that of his wife Nanna, who had died of grief, was brought onto Balder's famous ship, called Ringhorn (or Hringham), and set on fire. His ship, covered with treasures and flowers, was then sent out to sea, where it burned brightly before sinking. This became the model for Viking funerals at sea. No one would see the beloved Balder again, until Ragnarok, when he would be resurrected to begin the new world.

The Usefulness of Frey and Freya

At one point in Viking mythology, the Aesir gods decided to invite some of the Vanir gods to join them in Asgard as a gesture of good faith (although some versions of the story claim the Vanir were forced to appear). The two most important Vanir gods, Frey (or Freyr), the god of weather, the harvest, and peace, and his twin sister Freya, the goddess of love, sex, and beauty, joined them and quickly proved their worth. Frey became one of the Vikings' most important gods and, like Odin, was rewarded with human sacrifices. Frey proved he could be very useful to the other gods when he revealed his magic ship, called Skidbladnir, which was large enough to hold all the gods as it soared through water or air, but was also able to fold up so it fit in Frey's pocket. This helped the gods flee from dangerous situations.

Frey fell in love with a beautiful giantess named Gerd, and in exchange for his magic sword and his horse, his servant Skirnir agreed to woo Gerd for him. Gerd turned down all of Skirnir's offers. He finally had to threaten her life before she agreed to marry Frey.

In contrast, the beautiful Freya did not need to convince anyone to marry her. Gods, men, and giants alike all loved her. Her favorite possession was a precious necklace that she acquired by mating with the four dwarves who crafted it. Freya was quite free with her affections; emulating her, the Vikings engaged in raucous behavior, which included drinking a lot of ale and sexual promiscuity. She could also be very persuasive, and got Odin to agree that half of the warriors slain in battle (in addition to all women and children) would be hers

The Valkyries

The Valkyries (literally meaning "choosers of the slain") were goddesses of destiny. They appeared to warriors in their dreams the night before the warrior would die. Then during the battle they flew overhead on their white horses, dressed in full armor, and decided who would live and who would not.

After a warrior's death, the Valkyries escorted him to Odin's great hall, Valhalla, where they changed into white dresses and fed him wine for supper. Originally this group of women were represented as fierce and bloody demons of death, but they eventually became gentler and more beautified, with long blond hair and idealized bodies. They were then considered vulnerable to love, and the story of one fallen Valkyrie, Brunhild, showed that they would be willing to give their own life for the man they loved. The Greeks believed that the display of light shining off the Valkyries' shields explained the aurora borealis, the "northern lights" sometimes seen in the sky.

to take back to her own palace to rejoice, while he brought the other half of the dead warriors with him to Valhalla to feast and train for Ragnarok.

The End of an Era

By 1000 A.D., Christianity was beginning to take a strong hold on the Norse lands. Slowly the Vikings relinquished their deities and their myths, and in 1070 Iceland's national assembly officially declared Iceland a Christian country. By 1100, the Viking era of exploration and conquest had ended. For a period there was a blending of the two belief systems, as demonstrated by the archaeological discovery of artifacts like a replica of Thor's hammer with a Christian cross emblazoned on it.

Today, most of what is known about Norse mythology comes from two sources, both written as the Christian religion was eclipsing Viking culture. The *Elder Edda*, also called the *Poetic Edda*, is a collection of Old Norse verse written in the tenth and eleventh centuries. It is composed of thirty-four poems by various poets. The *Younger Edda*, also called the *Prose Edda*, is a collec-

A pendant representing Freya, the goddess of sex, love, and beauty. Around her neck is her prized necklace created by dwarfs.

The Origins of the Days of the Week

Some Norse gods have lent their names to the English days of the week:

Tuesday: Named for Tyr, based on a Germanic god named Tiw or Tiwaz
Wednesday: Named for Odin, also known as Wotan or Woden
Thursday: Named for Thor
Friday: Named for Frigga, although some argue the name derives from Freya

tion of myths and folklore written around 1220 by Icelandic scholar and politician Snorri Sturluson.

Today there is a revival of interest in the Norse myths, and Iceland has agreed to recognize the Nordic beliefs as a valid religion. Amid the raiding, plundering, conquering, and settling, the Vikings created a mythology that, in sheer complexity, rivaled any other in the ancient world.

Aztec Deities: Sacrifice for an Orderly Universe

Beginning as early as 1800 B.C., the Olmecs, the Zapotecs, the Maya, and the Toltecs all flourished in Mesoamerica, one civilization giving way to the next. Between them they built grand temples, carved intricate statues of their deities, waged war against their neighbors, created beautiful artifacts, and made advances in astronomy and mathematics. When the Aztecs settled the capitol city of Tenochtitlan (present-day Mexico City) in A.D. 1325, their dominance of the region began.

The Aztec leaders knew the transition to power would be easier if they assimilated some of the traditions and mythologies of the other cultures and neighboring tribes. This was also a sign of respect. The outcome of

this practice was that the Aztec pantheon of gods and goddesses eventually included some fifteen hundred deities of varying importance. This meant that many of the functions of the gods and goddesses overlapped. Earlier native cultures all believed that their gods had great control over their lives and must be worshiped, but the Aztecs took worship to a new level. Their views of the world and the structure of the universe demanded that the gods be appeased on a daily basis, and with great sacrifice. No other culture in recorded history worshiped its deities with the fervor, fortitude, and gusto of the Aztecs.

Mexico's central valley was prone to earthquakes, floods, and hurricanes, which fueled the Aztecs' fear that the earth was near collapse. Believing the gods were their only salvation against a harsh environment, they dutifully worshiped them by visiting public shrines and leaving food, art, and gold jewelry. They danced and sang at parades and festivals in the gods' honor, and sacrificed quail, dogs, turkeys, and an occasional jaguar to ensure the gods' favor. While that kind of worship was considered important, the gods exacted a much higher price for keeping the Aztecs' lives running smoothly and for ensuring the entire structure of the universe remained intact. That price, unfortunately for many, was blood. Not just the blood of animals, but the still-beating hearts of men, women, and children, sacrificed by various methods depending on the demands of the specific god or goddess.

The Structure of the Aztec Universe

The Aztecs justified the practice of human sacrifice in the belief that the entire universe was controlled by the gods, and that the Aztecs themselves were responsible for ensuring the gods did their jobs. For the gods to function, they needed the energy that only the life force of human blood could provide. The structure of the universe was very complicated, and it needed a lot of that life force to remain intact.

The Aztecs believed the cosmos was composed of three layers.

The top thirteen levels were the heavens, the nine lowest levels housed the underworld, and the earth was in the middle. Omeyocan was the name of the highest level of heaven where the god Ometeotl breathed life into the world. At the other extreme, Mictlantecuhtli, the lord of death, guarded Mictlan, the lowest level of the underworld. Each level of heaven and the underworld had a god or goddess associated with it. The

The magnificent capital city of Tenochtitlan was settled in A.D. 1325 by the powerful Aztec civilization.

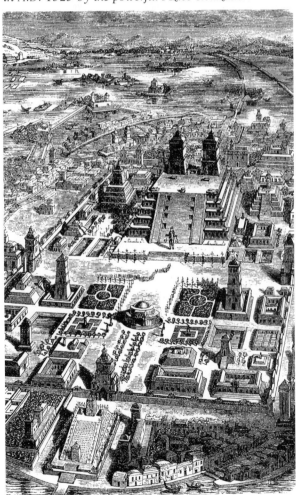

The Aztecs believed that the entire universe was controlled by the gods, who required the sacrifice of human blood to function.

earth itself was also divided into four horizontal sections, each associated with a different deity.

When they were not performing their duties, the gods and goddesses rested in a paradise called Tamoanchan, where it was always summer and food was always plentiful. Thought to be located either on a mountaintop nearly as high as the moon or on the highest level of heaven, this was where the gods originally made human beings, and where they went to escape the turmoil of the world.

Tenochtitlan rested in the middle of the four layers of Earth. In the center of the city lay the great double temple of Huitzilopochtli, the

Aztec national god, and Tlaloc, the rain god. The Aztecs believed that the oceans curled up to form the sky, and they feared that, should Tenochtitlan be captured or destroyed, the sky would fall down on them and the earth would be flooded. That scenario had supposedly already happened once before, and the gods had had to re-create the world and all its inhabitants. According to Aztec mythology, the universe had already been destroyed four times. The Aztecs believed they were now living on borrowed time since the gods could decide at any time to end the world again, and this time it would be permanent. They must do everything in their power to keep the gods happy and to keep themselves safe.

The Creator God Asks for Nothing

One supreme god existed outside of space and time and was known as Ometeotl, the lord of duality and sustenance. He was considered the source of all creation, who made the earth with his breath and watched over the world from the highest level of heaven. No temples were dedicated to him, as he was felt to be living in the hearths of each household. As his dual nature would suggest, he was actually both male and female, with the goddess Omecihuatl representing his female incarnation. Together they had

---

An Aztec Song in Response to the Conquest

This lament by an Aztec citizen is from the collection of Cantares Mexicanos housed in the National Library of Mexico, and was probably composed in 1523. It can be found on the Student Teacher Resource Center website.

The Fall of Tenochtitlan

*Our cries of grief rise up
and our tears rain down,
for Tlatelolco is lost.
The Aztecs are fleeing across the lake;
they are running away like women.*

*How can we save our homes, my people?
The Aztecs are deserting the city:
the city is in flames, and all
is darkness and destruction.*

*Motelchiuhtzin the Huiznahuacatl,
Tlacotzin the Tlailotlacatl,
Oquitzin the Tlacatecuhtli
are greeted with tears.*

*Weep, my people:
know that with these disasters
we have lost the Mexican nation.
The water has turned bitter,
our food is bitter!
These are the acts of the Giver of Life.*

four sons—Quetzalcoatl, Tezcatlipoca, Tlaloc, and Xipe Totec—who were each associated with one of the four cardinal directions on the earth.

As in Hindu mythology, these four gods were considered both deities in their own right and aspects of the one god. Ometeotl did not want the job of actually controlling the world, so he left that to his sons and their families. Quetzalcoatl, the god of wind and creation, took the job very seriously and became the most revered god of the Aztecs.

Quetzalcoatl and Creation

Beloved for his goodness, Quetzalcoatl was based on a god of the earlier Toltec people. The Aztecs believed this borrowed god gave them corn, taught them art and science, and showed them how to keep time. Associated with the planet Venus and the morning star, Quetzalcoatl's name translated as "the Plumed (feathered) Serpent" or "precious twin," and Quetzalcoatl indeed had a twin named Xolotl who usually appeared in the form of a dog.

A stone head of Quetzalcoatl, or "the Plumed Serpent," god of wind and creation.

Quetzalcoatl and his twin Xolotl played an integral role in the Aztec creation story. After the world had been destroyed for the fourth time, the two went down into the underworld. They asked Mictlantecuhtli, the god of death, for the bones of the humans who had lived before the destruction. Mictlantecuhtli did as they requested, but then sent quail to chase and torment the pair until they dropped the bones. Grabbing some fragments, they escaped back to Tamoanchan, where they sprinkled their own blood over the bones to make a new race of humans.

To create a home for the new humans, Quetzalcoatl's brother and greatest enemy, Tezcatlipoca, helped him stretch the body of the goddess Tlaltecuhtli across the earth to form the land, trees, and oceans. In reparation for the sacrifice of her body, the goddess demanded human hearts. So it is to the earth itself that the Aztecs felt their initial loyalty, and it was for her that they began the practice of human sacrifice.

Although there were many methods of sacrifice, the most common by far was to cut out the living victim's heart. The victim, often slightly intoxicated by a fermented drink called pulque, would be brought to the top of a temple and held down by priests on a sacrificial altar. The individual's heart would be cut out with a sharp flint, quartz, or obsidian knife and held up, still beating, for the gods to see. The heart would then be burned, while the body was pushed down the steep temple steps to be either dismembered or ceremoniously cut up and eaten. Though the victims of human sacrifice were believed to go to the highest level of heaven, few volun-

teered. Often the victims were prisoners of war from other neighboring tribes or villages. In fact, the Aztecs initiated wars they dubbed the Flower Wars, just for the purpose of increasing their supply of sacrifices. The Aztecs, not surprisingly, were not popular with their neighbors, who were often forced to watch the sacrifices take place.

Quetzalcoatl believed that a minor bloodletting was good enough for him, so many people chose to undergo a form of "autosacrifice" in his honor. They would stick a sharp tool through a fleshy area of their body, gather the resulting blood, and burn it in front of a representation of the god. The people took pride in the loyalty they could show their god. Tezcatlipoca was jealous of the people's love for Quetzalcoatl, and he tricked him into getting drunk and fleeing from the Aztec pantheon in disgrace. Quetzalcoatl promised to return one day from the east to resume his rightful position. When Spanish explorer Hernan Cortés arrived in Tenochtitlan in 1519, the people thought their beloved god had returned. Tezcatlipoca, however, would get the last laugh.

Because he could see the future, Tezcatlipoca, the god of destruction, the jaguar god of the night sky, was also called "the smoking mirror." Although he brought misfortune wherever he went, the forever youthful god was very popular, very important, and presided over warriors and princes. He also decided the fate of each child while it was still in its mother's womb.

One day Tezcatlipoca's destructive behavior reached across the boundaries of the Aztec kingdom to the Toltec city of Tollan

The Aztec Calendar System

The Aztecs kept two types of calendars simultaneously. The first one was 365 days long, and was divided into 20 months with 18 days per month. This left five days at the end of each year that were not a part of any month. These five days were considered bad luck, and people would stay in their houses and away from new enterprises during that time. Each month was associated with a few different deities, and festivals in their honor were held accordingly. The Aztecs did not take into account that the earth's revolution around the sun actually takes 365 1/4 days, not 365. This meant that without including a leap year every four years, their calendar eventually stopped accurately reflecting the changing of the seasons. Fortunately, they had another kind of calendar, called tonalpohualli, which helped them pinpoint dates with total accuracy.

Literally meaning "counting of the day-signs," this 260-day calendar didn't originate with the Aztecs, but they clung to it fiercely. Every single day of the 260 days was given a unique name, a number from 1 to 13, and one of twenty words associated with a deity. For example, the first day of a new cycle might be called One Wind, then the second would be Two Reed, and the third Three House, etc. Then after the 13th day, the cycle of numbers would start over, while the names would continue to cycle through until they reached the 20th. On the 261st day, the numbers and the words would catch up to each other and it would start over with One Wind. This unique calendar was used by fortune tellers who claimed to read the future with it, and babies were often named after the day they were born. Farmers used it to determine when to plant and when to harvest. Every 52 years, the 365-day calendar and the 260-day calendar would align, causing the Aztecs great fear and distress. They believed that on that day, the gods decided whether to preserve the world for another 52 years or destroy it.

(today known as Tula), at that time a thriving center. He tried to bring down the city by setting out to slay all its inhabitants. First he served a feast replete with singing and dancing. The god sang a song so fast that the dancers could not keep up. They went insane and were turned into rocks. In his quest to kill more of the citizenry, Tezcatlipoca disguised himself as a warrior and invited some townsfolk to visit his garden. Once the people entered the garden, the god attacked them with a garden hoe. Those who were not immediately slain were trampled in the mad dash to escape. Tezcatlipoca's next ruse was to venture to the city's marketplace, and there pretend he had a tiny child in his hand. When the curious flocked to see the child they were shocked to discover it was Tezcatlipoca's brother Huitzilopochtli, the god of war. But by that time, the crowd had grown so large that many were crushed to death. To finish off the rest of the city's inhabitants, Tezcatlipoca tricked the Toltecs into stoning him and Huitzilopochtli to death. Their bodies then expelled fumes deadly to all who touched them, including Tezcatlipoca and Huitzilopochtli. The gods were immortal and came back to life. The townsfolk were not so lucky.

In comparison with other deities like Huitzilopochtli, Coatlicue, Tlaloc, and Xipe Totec, Tezcatlipoca did not demand many sacrifices. He only had one stipulation—the men who were sacrificed in his honor had to be the most handsome in the land. According to Aztec scholar Inga Clendinnen:

> A young captive, chosen for his beauty, grace, and self-control impersonated Tezcatlipoca for an entire year. During this time, he was honored and lived a life of luxury and privilege. He was expected to wander the streets at night with his entourage, playing flutes and generally being congenial. Twenty days before the festival he was given four beautiful wives. At the beginning of the festival, he was taken quietly to a temple on a small island where, at a time of his own choosing, his heart was cut out and offered to Tezcatlipoca.[7]

Huitzilopochtli and Coatlicue

When Huitzilopochtli was not being led around by Tezcatlipoca, he fulfilled his job as the sun god and the god of war. As the sun god, he had the most important role in the whole Aztec pantheon and was considered the Aztecs' patron god. His physical appearance also set him apart; he had blue skin with hummingbird feathers tied around one leg. Hummingbirds, believed to be the souls of dead warriors, accompanied Huitzilopochtli as he carried the sun each day across the sky. He is credited with leading the Aztecs to Tenochtitlan, and the city is dedicated to him. The story of Huitzilopochtli's birth by the son of the earth goddess Coatlicue was one of the Aztecs' most famous myths.

Coatlicue was a fearful goddess who lived on a diet of corpses. She was depicted with clawed feet and two serpent heads, wearing a vest of human skin or snakes and a necklace

A statue of the earth goddess Coatlicue, who was believed to live on a diet of corpses.

of hearts, skulls, and severed hands. One day some white feathers fell from the sky and she tucked them into her dress. Much to the horror of her four hundred sons and one daughter, this act made her pregnant. Her children plotted to kill her so she would not disgrace them with her pregnancy. She was scared, but her unborn son Huitzilopochtli told her to hide. The warning came too late, however, and her children attacked her and chopped off her head. At that moment Huitzilopochtli sprang from his mother's body, fully formed and armed with weapons. He decapitated his sister and flung her head into the sky, where it became the moon. He then killed his four hundred brothers, who became the stars.

Human sacrifice was believed to be the only way to guarantee that Huitzilopochtli would continue to make the sun rise each morning. Although sacrifices to him were conducted on a daily basis, he is best known for the events that took place in 1487. The Aztecs decided to rededicate the Great Temple in the center of Tenochtitlan, which Huitzilopochtli shared with Tlaloc, the god of rain. For the ceremony, the Aztec warriors captured tens of thousands of prisoners, and one by one they were marched to the top of the Great Temple and had their hearts ripped out. Historians conclude as many as 80,000 men, women, and children were massacred during the four-day ceremony in honor of Huitzilopochtli and his mother Coatlicue.

Cruelty in the Name of Tlaloc and Xipe Totec

The importance of the gods who controlled the weather and the crops in this agricultural

society cannot be overestimated. Tlaloc could be called on to provide rain in a drought, and to stop rain during floods. His role as provider of rain and running water was so vital to the Aztecs that in order to prove their devotion, the priests sacrificed babies and young children in his name. The harder the children cried, the better the rainy season for the crops as their tears symbolized rain. Most of the children were between the ages of eight and twelve, but some were newborns. Rather than having the priests remove the children's hearts, Tlaloc often demanded a different death of his sacrificial victims: their heads were chopped off.

Another ritual for Tlaloc took place once a year and involved his wife (sometimes referred to as his sister) Chalchiuhtlicue, the goddess of the seas who helped the crops grow and protected newborn babies. Each year during the dry season (spring), a young woman would dress as Chalchiuhtlicue and wait for the priests to arrive. She was then sacrificed and her blood was poured into the lake.

The god of crops, springtime, and planting, Xipe Totec was also particular about the manner in which his sacrificial victims died. He was believed to have suffered greatly in his job of bringing springtime to the world, so his sacrificial victims, in turn, must suffer greatly as well. The priests performed two kinds of sacrifice to this important god. Often, his victims were flayed (their skin peeled off to symbolize a husk of corn being sheared) and their skins given to others to wear around town, bloody- side out. Sometimes the victims were bound to a board and

A statue of Xipe Totec, the god of crops, springtime, and planting, dressed in the skin of a sacrificial victim.

shot through with arrows until they bled to death, their blood making the ground fertile and symbolizing falling rain. The goddess Chicomecoatl was the female aspect of corn, and thereby associated with Xipe Totec. Her sacrificial victims, young girls, were also flayed or decapitated.

Xochiquetzal and Tlazolteotle

Two other Aztec goddesses, Xochiquetzal and Tlazolteotle, represented opposing views of women and their place in society. Xochiquetzal, the fertility goddess, personified the female traits of beauty, kindness, and grace. Associated with pleasure, childbirth, the arts, and flowers, she was paired with many differ-

ent gods. At one point she was abducted by either Tezcatlipoca or Xolotl and taken to the underworld. She ate from the tree of sexual knowledge, and as a result sexual pleasure was brought into the world. Sacrifices to Xochiquetzal usually took the form of young virgin women who had their hearts cut out. During an annual celebration called the Feast of Flowers, one young virgin dressed as Xochiquetzal was flayed, and the priest wearing her skin would sit at the foot of the temple pretending to weave cloth.

Depicted as a comely young woman, Xochiquetzal is the opposite of her fellow goddess Tlazolteotle, who symbolized sexual lust. She was called the "eater of filth," and was personified as a haglike creature wearing the skin of her sacrifices. She could absolve sinners, so many Aztecs late in life confessed their sins to her in the hopes of being purified before they died. Her sacrifices were in the form of young women forced into prostitution before being killed in a ritual ceremony.

A Sudden End

While searching for gold in what is today known as the Central Valley of Mexico, the Spanish explorer Hernan Cortés and his troops first stumbled on the Aztec city of Tenochtitlan in early November 1519. The conquistadors were amazed by its glory and by the accomplishments of a civilization unlike any they had ever seen. The city, with its complex of stone temples, elaborate courtyards, small islands, and five square miles of canals rose out of the center of Lake Texcoco. With a population larger than any European city at that time, Tenochtitlan was connected to the mainland by a number of causeways, which allowed the Spanish conquerors easy access.

At first the Aztec ruler Montezuma welcomed Cortés, because he believed Cortés was the beloved god Quetzalcoatl returning to them as had been prophesied. In the name of spreading Christianity to a heathen society, the Spanish soldiers knocked down tem-

ples, destroyed sacred statues, and ended the traditional worship of the Aztec gods and goddesses.

The Aztecs tried to convince the Spanish conquerors that they must be allowed to continue making sacrifices to their deities, or else terrible things would happen. Their arguments were not taken seriously, however, and Christianity soon took a stronghold in the

An illustration of the meeting between Cortés and Aztec ruler Montezuma. Montezuma welcomed the Spanish conqueror because he believed Cortés was the god Quetzalcoatl returning to Earth as prophesied.

Journey into the Afterlife

The Aztec vision of the afterlife was bleak. The soul's destination, whether one of the upper levels of heaven or the lower levels of the underworld, depended not on how well they had lived their life, but on the circumstances surrounding their death. To achieve heaven, one must die a hero's death in battle, in childbirth, or as part of an important sacrifice. If one's life ended through an act of nature—like lightning or floods—one would wind up in the level of heaven ruled by Tlaloc, the rain god. Everyone else would surely wind up in Mictlan, the underworld, although the journey there was fraught with danger. The dead were buried (or cremated) with supplies thought to help them make it through the levels of the underworld with greater ease. If the deceased was an important man in society, his wife and servants might be killed to travel alongside him. Once the person died, he was expected to have to face the gods of the underworld and pass their insidious tests. With the guidance of a yellow dog, they had to scale cliffs, cross rushing waters, fight dragons, avoid speeding knives, and more, only to make it to the lowest level of Mictlan, where the god of death, Mictlantecuhtli, awaited them.

entire valley of Mexico. Rather than completely abandoning their gods, the Aztecs combined the stories of the Christian saints and heroes with their own mythology to form deities who are still worshiped today. It had taken thousands of years for the Aztec civilization to arise out of the previous native Mesoamerican societies. It only took seven hundred soldiers with sixteen horses two years to destroy it.

Notes

Introduction: The Origins of the Gods

1. Carl G. Jung, *Alchemical Studies,* in *The Collected Works of C. G. Jung,* vol. 13, Bollingen Series XX. Princeton, NJ: Princeton University Press, 1967.
2. Roni Jay, *Teach Yourself Mythology.* Chicago: NTC, 1996, pp. 3–4.

Chapter One: Egytian Deities: The Duality of Nature

3. Mary Barnett, *Gods and Myths of Ancient Egypt.* New York: Smithmark, 1996, p. 34.

Chapter Two: Hindu Deities: 333 Million Manifestations of Divinity

4. Charles Phillips, Michael Kerrigan, and David Gould, *The Eternal Cycle: Indian Myth.* London: Duncan Baird Publishers, 1998, p. 27.

Chapter Three: Celtic Deities: A Love of High Adventure

5. Peter Berresford Ellis, *Dictionary of Celtic Myth.* New York: Oxford University Press, 1992, p. 14.
6. Charles Squire, *Celtic Myths and Legends.* New York: Grammercy, 1994, p. 40.

Chapter Seven: Aztec Deities: Sacrifice for an Orderly Universe

7. Inga Clendinnen, *Aztecs: An Interpretation.* Cambridge, England: Cambridge University Press, 1991, pp. 104–10.

For Further Reading

Thomas Bulfinch, *Bulfinch's Mythology*, New York: Random House, 1993. Although written nearly 150 years ago, this resource is still a valuable link of mythology with literature and art.

Arthur Cotterell, *The Encylopedia of Mythology*. New York: Smithmark, 1996. Really three books in one, Cotterell examines the gods and heroes of Classical (Greek and Roman), Celtic, and Norse mythology.

Proinsias Mac Cana, *Celtic Mythology*. New York: Peter Bedrick Books, 1985. Along with many photographs of ancient artifacts, this book offers background on the Celtic people and insights into their mythology.

Kevin Crossley-Holland, *The Norse Myths*. New York: Pantheon, 1980. The author first presents a history of the Norse myth and then relates thirty-two classic tales interwoven with commentary.

Edith Hamilton, *Mythology*. New York: New American Library, 1940. A still-valuable and important classic text that matter-of-factly relays Greek, Roman, and Norse mythologies.

Nancy Hathaway, *The Friendly Guide to Mythology*. New York: Viking Press, 2001. This wonderfully engaging book looks at mythological characters from cultures all over the world.

Peter Kamara, *Ancient Roman Mythology*. Edison, NJ: Chartwell Books, 1996. Along with beautiful photographs of Roman sculptures, paintings, and buildings, the author offers a concise discussion of ancient Roman life and religion followed by encyclopedic entries of important Roman mythological characters.

Sheila Keenan, *Gods, Goddesses, and Monsters*. New York: Scholastic, 2000. This accessible book offers encyclopedic entries of mythological characters from various cultures, along with related interesting facts about the mythological history of that culture.

Charles Phillips, Michael Kerrigan, and David Gould, *The Eternal Cycle: Indian Myth*. London: Duncan Baird, 1998. An excellent work that explores Hindu and Buddhist history and mythology through tales of their gods and goddesses.

Works Consulted

Books

Tony Allan and Tom Lowenstein, *Gods of Sun and Sacrifice: Aztec & Maya Myth*. London: Duncan Baird, 1997. This book is an indispensable, in-depth study of Aztec and Mayan deities, myths, and rituals.

Mary Barnett, *Gods and Myths of Ancient Egypt*. New York: Smithmark, 1996. An overview of the Egyptian gods that is aimed at young adults.

———, *Gods and Myths of the Romans*. New York: Smithmark, 1996. Another fine overview directed at younger readers.

David Bellingham, *An Introduction to Greek Mythology*. Secausus, NJ: Chartwell Books, 1989. The author presents a focused examination of the births and relationships of the Greek gods and heroes.

Juan Alberto Roman Berrelleaza, "Sacrifice of Children at the Great Temple," *Mexican Archaeology*, vol. 6, no. 31, May/June 1998. This article relays an archaeological report of data uncovered at an excavation of the Aztec's Great Temple in modern Mexico City.

Arthur Gilchrist Brodeur, trans., *The Prose Edda*, by Snorri Sturluson. London: Oxford University Press, 1916. Brodeur offers a solid translation of Icelandic medieval historian/poet Sturluson's collection of Norse myths.

Alfonso Caso, *The Aztecs: People of the Sun*. Tulsa: University of Oklahoma Press, 1967. This is a reader-friendly analysis of Aztec myth and ritual written by the Director of Archaeology of the National Museum of Mexico, and features illustrations by the famed Mexican artist Miguel Covarrubias.

R.T. Rundle Clark, *Myth and Symbol in Ancient Egypt*. London: Thames and Hudson, 1969. This scholarly presentation investigates the roots of Egyptian religion and myth from a historical and psychological viewpoint.

Peter Clayton, *Great Figures of Mythology*. New York: Crescent Books, 1990. This "coffee-table" book highlights photographs of classical statues and artwork, along with descriptions of the major characters of world mythology.

Inga Clendinnen, *Aztecs: An Interpretation*. Cambridge, England: Cambridge University Press, 1991. The esteemed author recreates Aztec life by using historical data to paint a greater understanding of the society's motivations.

Malcolm Couch, *Greek and Roman Mythology*. New York: Todtri, 1997. Couch offers an informative study of the history of Classical mythology and its deities.

H. R. Ellis Davidson, *Gods and Myths of Northern Europe*. Baltimore: Penguin Books, 1964. Davidson's important, scholarly overview of Norse mythology is based on the few sources left behind.

Romesh C. Dutt, trans., *The Rama-yana and the Maha-bharata*. New York: E. P. Dutton, 1910. This is a very readable translation of two of the most treasured ancient texts in the Hindu religion.

Alexander Eliot, *The Universal Myths*. New York: NAL/Penguin, 1990. Eliot reveals common themes and mythic structures that run through several ancient and modern religions.

Peter Berresford Ellis, *Dictionary of Celtic Myth*. New York: Oxford University Press, 1992.

Novelist and historian Peter Ellis writes short but engaging dictionary entries regarding people, places, and events in Celtic myth.

Raymond Faulkner, trans., *The Egyptian Book of the Dead*. San Francisco: Chronicle Books, 1994. Featuring very clear color photographs of an ancient copy of the *Papyrus of Ani* (now known as *The Book of the Dead*), this is an important translation and presentation of the spiritual and philosophical teachings of ancient Egypt.

Hesiod, *Theogony, The Works and Days, The Shield of Herakles*. Trans. Richmond Lattimore. Ann Arbor: University of Michigan Press, 1991. In readable verse, Lattimore translates these three landmark works of the ancient Greek epic poet Hesiod.

Homer, *The Homeric Hymns*. Trans. Apostolos N. Athanassakis. Baltimore Johns Hopkins University Press, 1976. Scholarly notes and explanations serve as valuable companions to this version of the hymns collected by the ancient Greek poet Homer.

Garry Hogg, *Cannibalism and Human Sacrifice*. New York: Citadel, 1966. An older volume on the practice of human sacrifice in many cultural and religious settings.

Roni Jay, *Teach Yourself Mythology*. Chicago: NTC, 1996. An easy-to-follow basic introduction to the mythologies of many ancient cultures, this guide also includes brief descriptions of the deities.

Gwyn Jones and Thomas Jones, trans., *The Mabinogion*. Rutland, VT: Charles E. Tuttle, 1993. With a preface by author John Updike, this version does an excellent job of relaying the eleven tales of this medieval collection of Welsh myths.

Carl G. Jung, *Alchemical Studies,* in *The Collected Works of C. G. Jung,* vol. 13, Bollingen Series XX. Princeton, NJ: Princeton University Press, 1967. Five essays by psychoanalytic theorist Carl Jung. While ostensibly dealing with the ancient art of alchemy, Jung's work traces the link between spiritual beliefs and modern psychology.

Jean Mascaro, trans., *The Bhagavad Gita*. Middlesex, England: Penguin Books, 1962. Sanskrit scholar Mascaro offers a concise interpretation of the ancient Hindu text that conveys the text's spiritual message.

Marilyn McFarlane, *Sacred Myths: Stories of World Religions*. Portland, OR: Sibyl, 1996. This retelling of thirty-five classic stories and sacred myths from seven world religions is accompanied by rich computer-based artwork.

Michael C. Meyer and William L. Sherman, *The Course of Mexican History*. 5th ed. New York: Oxford University Press, 1995. This volume serves as the leading comprehensive study of the history of Mexico from the pre-Columbian period to the present.

Ovid, *Metamorphoses*. Trans. Horace Gregory. New York: New American Library, 1958. Gregory offers an enjoyable translation of Ovid's tales of Roman mythology.

Neil Philip, *Myths and Legends*. New York: DK, 1999. Clear, concise text accompanies beautiful reproductions of ancient statues and artifacts.

Charles Squire, *Celtic Myths and Legends*. New York: Grammercy, 1994. Although originally written in the early twentieth century, this is still one of the most comprehensive studies of Celtic myth, legend, and poetry ever produced.

Virgil, *The Aeneid*. Trans. John Dryden. New York: Limited Editions Club/Heritage Press, 1944. This famous translation does justice to Virgil's epic story of Aeneas, the founder of ancient Rome.

Madhu Bazaz Wangu, *Hinduism*. New York: Facts On File, 1991. Wangu presents the history, customs, and beliefs of Hinduism while describing the mysteries and myths that sustained its growth over the centuries.

Internet Sources

Encyclopedia Mythica is a sizable database of more than five thousand seven hundred definitions of gods and goddesses, supernatural beings, legendary creatures, and monsters from all over the world. http://www.pantheon.org/mythica.html.

The Book of Gods, Goddesses, Heroes, and other Characters of Mythology is a compilation of information about all aspects of mythology. http://www.cybercomm.net/~grandpa/gdsindex.html.

The Perseus Digital Library provides full or partial texts of many ancient books, plays, and poems. The site is maintained by the Department of Classics at Tufts University. http://www.perseus.tufts.edu.

Student Teacher Resource Center provides extensive educational information on the history of Mexico and the Aztecs for both students and teachers. http://northcoast.com/~spdtom/index.html.

Index

Picture Credits

About the Author

Wendy Mass is currently finishing a Doctor of Letters degree at Drew University in Madison, New Jersey. She holds an M.A. in Creative Writing from California State University, Long Beach, and a B.A. in English from Tufts University. She is the cofounder of *Writes of Passage*, a national literary journal for teenagers, and the author of both fiction and nonfiction books for young adults.